PERCEPTIONS OF DEVELOPING CULTURAL AWARENESS OF FIRST-LEVEL HIGH SCHOOL ARABIC LANGUAGE LEARNERS

Nabila Hammami
and
Ashraf Esmail

University Press of America,® Inc.
Lanham · Boulder · New York · Toronto · Plymouth, UK

Copyright © 2014 by
University Press of America,® Inc.
4501 Forbes Boulevard
Suite 200
Lanham, Maryland 20706
UPA Acquisitions Department (301) 459-3366

10 Thornbury Road
Plymouth PL6 7PP
United Kingdom

All rights reserved

British Library Cataloging in Publication Information Available

Library of Congress Control Number: 2013951354
ISBN: 978-0-7618-6247-5 (paperback :   paper)
eISBN: 978-0-7618-6248-2

This book is dedicated to the family of Nabila Hammami
To her mother, *Haniya Jaber-Barada,*
In honor of her uniquely gifted love
And lack of literacy skills
That was the foundation of all Nabila's knowledge and existence
The memory of Nabila's most humble and loving father,
Moussa Barada,
Who was determined to teach himself how to read and write
Nabila's most beautiful homeland, *Lebanon,*
For allowing Nabila to survive throughout the war years
Nabila's **brothers:** *Nabil, Suleiman, Mohammad, & Ali*
Sharers of all delights & sorrows
Nabila's **sisters-in-law:** *Ahlam, Tahani, & Maha*
Who love Nabila any way
Nabila's **wonderful** *nephews & nieces*
For loving their aunt unconditionally
Nabila's most precious sons, *Shaam & Jude,*
Without whom she could not be a real mother
To an *April* day

CONTENTS

Tables	vii
Figures	ix
Preface	xi
Foreword	xiii
Chapter One—Introduction to the Study	1
Chapter Two—Literature Review	13
Chapter Three—Methodology	39
Chapter Four—Results	53
Chapter Five—Discussion and Recommendations	68
References	81
Index	92

TABLES

Table 1.1. Most Widely Spoken Languages in the World   2
Table 1.2. Fall 1998, 2002, and 2006 Language Enrollment in U.S. Colleges   2
Table 4.1. Themes and Subthemes   55
Table 4.2. Themes   56
Table 4.3. Theme 1: Connecting Language and Culture   57
Table 4.4. Theme 2: Developing Culture Learning   59
Table 4.5. Theme 3: Improving Culture Learning and Teaching   63

FIGURES

Figure 2.1. The Five Cs of Foreign Language Study   20
Figure 2.2. The Interdependence of the Three Ps   22
Figure 2.3. The Socioeducational Model   29
Figure 3.1. Qualitative Data Analysis   49
Figure 3.2. Process of Data Analysis in this Qualitative Case Study   50

PREFACE

The role of the Arabic language today can hardly be overstated. It is the official language of over twenty countries with well over 300 million native speakers making it the fifth most commonly spoken native language in the world. While there continues to be an extreme shortage of people in the West who are versed the Arabic language and culture, the demand for Arabic speakers has experienced an increase after the wars, the tragic events of 9/11 and the Israeli- Palestinian crises. These events, as well as the growing importance of the Middle East in international affairs, have led the American government to position Arabic as a language of strategic importance in order to promote cultural integration and make up for perceived weaknesses in linguistic and cultural competences in the language.

Teaching Arabic as a world language has therefore been introduced into certain school districts with Arab American representation. However, the teaching method, which involved grammatical rules and memorization, was centered on the learner's experience and did not produce desirable results or increase the learner's interest in the language. A new approach was introduced which incorporated the cultural context of the Arab language into the learning process. This approach focused not only on the learners but also on the teachers and the extent to which they understood the cultural and ethnic standards of the language. In order to ascertain and promote the connection between language development and cultural learning, this study investigates the challenges that characterize Arabic cultural awareness and how Arab American high school teachers have improved their students' learning ability by introducing them to different aspects of the Arab culture.

The study uses the qualitative analyses method by conducting interviews with five Arab language teachers in two high schools of a district with high Arab American representation. The purpose was to get their perceptions regarding linguistic development for first-level learners through cultural awareness. This research identifies language and culture as major components in world language instruction and reveals that learning a language can take place when the learners use different tools and characteristics of the sociocultural environment of the language to communicate with each other under the guidance of their teachers or adults.

The conceptual framework for this study is based on two theories: Vygotsky's sociocultural theory and Gardner's socioeducational theory. The first concentrates on the learner's ability to endure meaningful communication with individuals in different social settings and, by such mediation, progress into more advanced levels of the language (Vygotsky, 1987). However, the second specifies that while language acquisition can take place in formal and informal settings, the outcome also depends on the learners' attitude towards wanting to adopt the behavioral aspects of the host language as well the learners' motivation, language anxiety and learning strategy (Gardner, 2006).

The literature review describes these theories as well as specifications of Arab language education and culture. Chapter Three follows with an explanation of the qualitative method used for this study in order to obtain different investigational perspectives and opinions about the issue; and the findings in Chapter Four indicate that cultural awareness greatly helps first level learners of the Arabic language. Chapter Five concludes with recommendations for future research.

The benefits of learning the Arabic language are considerable, and range from global and cultural acceptance to economic development. The United States like many other nations is looking for ways to ensure availability of quailfied, competent and effective Arab language teaching staff. This study is an important step towards this goal and represents a must read because it demonstrates the use of cultural awareness as a tool to facilitate the Arab language learning process.

Adnan Omar, Ph.D
Southern University at New Orleans

REFERENCES

Gardner, R. C. (2006). The socio-educational model of second language acquisition: A research paradigm. *EUROSLA Yearbook, 6,* 237–260.

Vygotsky, L.S. (1929). The problem of the cultural development of the child, II. *Journal of Genetic Psychology,* (36), 414–434.

FOREWORD

As an African American Teacher/Professor, who has taught and was educated at both ends of the educational spectrum, I am well aware of the importance of understanding students' cultural backgrounds in order to help them reach their fullest potential. Educators must be able to connect with their students' **cultural backgrounds** in order to make learning meaningful and real. When teachers understand the cultural backgrounds of their students, their knowledge will enable them to make the educational process a more meaningful and interesting experience for all students. Before teachers can impact the educational process, teachers must have an understanding of their own cultural identities, and the impact of their beliefs and educational goals of all students (Hilliard, 2001; Wilson, 1991). There must be a connection between the text and the students. In their research, Drs. Nabila Hammami and Ashraf Esmail, clearly explain the interrelatedness of the five C's (Communication, Cultures, Connections, Comparisons, and Communities) as well as the three components of the Arabic culture known as the three P's **(Practices, Products, and Perspectives)**. Even though students may have the same nationality and ethnic background, they all have different experiences, and educators must be able to meet and address all students' **social and educational needs**.

Because schools all across the United States are becoming more diverse, it is essential for teachers to gain an understanding of diversity beyond race and ethnicity. Cultural competence is fundamental if educators are to teach the diverse population of students in our schools (Hodgkinson, 1987). Therefore, teachers must have a firm understanding of the definition of cultural competence. As defined by Cross et al. (1989) and Isaacs and Benjamin (1991), cultural competence is a set of similar behaviors, attitudes, and policies that combine in an agency, a system, or among professionals, enabling those groups to work effectively in cross-cultural situations.

A study conducted by Morrier, Irving, Dandy, Dmitriyev, and Ukeje (2007) supported previous research efforts which demonstrated teachers' lack of cultural awareness decrease the academic achievement of minority students (Hudson et al., 2003; Serwatka, Deering, & Grants, 1995; Thompson et al., 2004). It is evident that higher education institutions must provide extra training and educational support to assist teachers in comprehending and accepting diversity as a way of life because they will never know who will cross the threshold of their classroom door. Therefore, preparation is "key." Without proper training, academic gaps will still exist among cultures, regardless of the content being taught.

In order for teachers to be successful in their classrooms, it is incumbent upon the university faculty who train teachers to embrace diversity, as well as demonstrate their competence and awareness of diversity to effectively train the twenty-first century teachers for the classroom. Researchers have identified the following cultural identities: race, ethnicity/nationality, social class, sex/gender, health, age, geographic region, sexuality, religion, social status, language and ability/disability. These identities are present in all cultures around the world, and they influence how people and educators treat, think, feel, judge, and for the most part teach individuals.

Shawan O. Bellow, Ed.D.
Assistant Professor and Interim Chair of Elementary Education
Southern University at New Orleans

References

Cross, T., et al (1989). *Towards a culturally competent system of care, volume I*. Washington, D.C.: Georgetown University Child Development Center, CASSP Technical Assistance Center.

Hilliard, A. G., III. (2001). Race, identity, hegemony and education: What do we need to know now? In Watkins, W., Lewis, J. H., and Chou, V. (Eds.), *Race and education: The roles of history and society in the education of African-American students*. Boston: Allyn and Bacon.

Hodgkinson, H.L. (1987, Summer) Changing society: Unchanging curriculum. *National Forum: Phi Kappa Phi Journal*, 67(3), 3-7.

Hudson, C. M., Brown, C., Belcher, J., Cleveland, W., Cox, W., Dunning, A., et al. (2003). *Report of the research and policy analysis subcommittee*. Atlanta, GA: The University System of Georgia's Task Force on Enhancing Access for African American Males.

Isaacs, M. & Benjamin, M. (1991). *Towards a culturally competent system of care, volume II, programs which utilize culturally competent principles*. Washington, D.C.: Georgetown University Child Development Center, CASSP Technical Assistance Center.

Morrier, M., Irving, M.A., Dandy, E., Dmitriyev, G., and Ukeje, I.C. (2007, Spring). Teaching and learning within and across cultures: Educator requirements across the United States. *Multicultural Education*, 14(3), 32, Retrieved March 10, 2008, from ProQuest database.

CHAPTER ONE
INTRODUCTION TO THE STUDY

Introduction

In the shadow of the tragic events of the terrorist attacks of September 11, 2001, the federal government has required that U.S. schools encourage American students to learn critically-needed languages, such as Arabic, in order to strengthen national security and be economically competitive with the rest of the world. The essential purpose for stimulating foreign language learning was to "foster global and cultural understanding essential to maintaining "a conducive environment for peace and prosperity" (Taha, 2006, p. 151). The U.S. government thought that the whole nation was facing critical deficiencies in foreign languages and that national weakness was the lack of government agents who were linguistically and culturally competent in two languages (Cutshall, 2007).

The interest in learning Arabic in the United States increased dramatically after the tragic events of 9/11 (Husseinali, 2006; Samimy, 2008). In fact, enrollment in Arabic courses throughout the United States "doubled from 5,500 in 1998 up to 10,600 in 2002" (Cutshall, 2007, p. 32). According to a nationwide survey of K–12 schools conducted by the National Capital Language Resource Center, "at least 18 public and charter schools currently teach Arabic as part of their regular foreign language curriculum" (National Standards for Foreign Language Education Project [National Standards], 2006, p. 115). According to Cutshall (2007), Arabic is the "fifth language world wide, the language of the Qur'an, the sixth in the United Nations, and the eleventh most spoken language in the United States" (p. 32). However, the Modern Language Association (2009) reported that Arabic is the tenth most taught language in the United States. Table 1.1 shows the most widely spoken languages in the world, while Table 1.2 indicates the most studied languages in the United States.

Table 1.1
Most Widely Spoken Languages in the World

Language	No. Speakers
Chinese (Mandarin)	1,075,000,000
English	514,000,000
Hindustania	496,000,000
Spanish	425,000,000
Russian	275,000,000
Arabic	256,000,000
Bengali	215,000,000
Portuguese	194,000,000
Malay-Indonesian	176,000,000
French	129,000,000

Note. Adapted from *Most Widely Spoken Languages in the World*, by Fact Monster, 2012. Copyright 2007 by Pearson. Retrieved from http://www.factmonster.com/ipka/ A0775272. html.

Table 1.2
Fall 1998, 2002, and 2006 Language Enrollment in U.S. Colleges

2006 Ranking and Language		1998	2002	% Change '98-'02	2006	% Change '02-'06
1	Spanish	656,590	746,267	+13.7	822,985	+10.3
2	French	199,064	201,979	+1.5	206,426	+2.2
3	German	89,020	91,100	+2.3	94,264	+3.5
4	American Sign	11,420	60,781	+432.2	78,829	+29.7
5	Italian	49,287	63,899	+29.6	78,368	+22.6
6	Japanese	43,141	52,238	+21.1	66,605	+27.5
7	Chinese	28,456	34,153	+20.0	51,582	+51.0
8	Latin	26,145	29,841	+14.1	32,191	+7.9
9	Russian	23,791	23,921	+0.5	24,845	+3.9
10	Arabic	5,505	10,584	+923.3	23,974	+126.5

Note. Adapted from "New MLA survey shows significant increases in foreign language study at U.S. colleges and universities", by Modern Language Association (2009). Copyright 2012 by Modern Language Association

Moreover, the devastating attacks of 9/11 were significant because they made Arab Americans and Muslims targets of hate crimes, discrimination, hostility, bigotry, and racism (Wingfield, 2006). Worse than that, they became "confronted by ethnic stratification and cultural invisibility" (p. 255). That perception forced the Arab American community to fight fiercely for the survival of the Arabic language in the school districts where Arab Americans reside because Arabic was, and still is, a symbol of their pride, culture, and ethnicity. In fact, the term *Arab* is not only a cultural term but also a linguistic one. The Arabic community is brought together by its unique culture and rich history. Ayouby (2004) stated that Arabic is not only the Arab American community's "religious link but also a vehicle for the preservation of a sense of a particularistic identity, especially among the young, who would be its learners" (p. 226). To that end, various K–12 Arabic courses were developed because of "significant numbers of heritage language speakers in the schools, even though the intent was to teach Arabic as a foreign language" (National Standards, 2006, p. 115). In other words, the Arabic programs offered in the schools that are located in one large metropolitan city had to accommodate heritage students who had varying degrees of linguistic and cultural backgrounds as well as Arab American students learning Arabic as a foreign language for the first time.

The current study included two of the high schools within one of the metropolitan school districts that has "nearly 900 of the 17,700 Arab American students studying Arabic as a foreign language—that is the highest number for any public school district in the country," as Zehr(2006, p. 7) indicated. Teaching Arabic as a world language has been introduced in the two public schools as a full educational matrix out of the need to connect with students' lives, experiences, identities, and practices. It is important to note that the bloody civil war that erupted in Lebanon in 1975 and lasted for 17 years, the two Gulf wars, and the Israeli-Palestinian conflict, served in the development of a unique Arabic program at the high school level, even though it was not influential enough to attract students of non-Arabic backgrounds. Still, the overwhelming expansion in student enrollment in Arabic classes at the high school level necessitated a supportive curriculum that spoke well to the needs and demands of the Arab American community with various diversities and ethnic backgrounds (Cutshall, 2005).

Thus, acknowledging the importance of preserving, improving, restoring, and reconnecting with Arabic language and culture (Wingfield, 2006) led to the development of the Standards for Learning Arabic in 2006 by almost 13 national, state, and local educators and researchers. The foreign language standards "show students, parents, and policy makers what students should know and be able to do after a longer sequence of study" (National Standards, 2006, p. 100). From a broad perspective, the Standards for Learning Arabic were created in order to transcend class instruction from the traditional way, where rote memorization of vocabulary and grammar rules dominated, to the nontraditional practice, where the learning becomes totally student-centered and more communicative. Bollag (2008) stated that "adults learn a new language the same way little children do—by exploiting innate abilities in order to communicate with those around them" (p. 57). The Arabic standards identified five essential components reflected in the five competencies (five Cs) articulated in the National Standards of Foreign Language Learning in the twenty-first century. Those learning standards are "Communication, Cultures, Connections, Comparisons, and Communities" (National Standards, 2006, p. 9). The current study, however, focused on the standard of *culture* because learning a foreign language requires real face-to-face interaction or communication with others; however, because communication is at the heart of all language study, it cannot be mastered without considering the cultural meanings in which the target/Arabic language occurs. Ketchum (2006) stated that "the written word in particular, taken devoid of its cultural and interpersonal context, can lead to vast misunderstandings easily avoidable through a culturally informed approach to textual communication" (p. 22). Hence, culture becomes the ultimate goal of Arabic as a foreign language, and its language is what learners use to reach that goal.

Problem Statement

Although the five area goals articulated in the National Standards (2006) for learning foreign languages—communication, cultures, connections, comparisons, and communities—are so intertwined and interconnected in the K–12 learning environment, absent from the literature are investigations on how K–12 teachers are able to implement and incorporate the practices, products, and perspectives of culture into world language classrooms in the United States. In fact, while world language teachers may be able to find clear examples of culture-specific practices (e.g., greetings) or products (e.g., foods), "most teachers lack sufficient background knowledge and experience to determine relationships between those practices and products and the cultural perspectives (e.g., values) that give rise to them" (Schulz, 2007, p. 10). Thus, the researchers were unsure if Arab American high school teachers of Arabic have developed students' cultural awareness through the perspectives, practices, and products of Arabic culture.

In addition, while the literature indicated that language and culture are essential components of foreign/world language instruction, it failed to show that high school teachers of Arabic have integrated culture in their beginning Arabic courses. Despite the high emphasis on the standards in the field of Arabic as a foreign language, the standards "do not prescribe what students of the target language should know and be able to do at the end of high school" (National Standards, 2006, p. 27). In addition, considerable attention has been given to what learners can do in a foreign language classroom, but "very little attention has been placed on what their teachers should know and be able to do as foreign language educators" (McAlpine& Dhonau, 2007, p. 248). Hence, it was the intent of this researcher to allow teachers of Arabic to see and seek the connections between Arabic language learning and culture learning.

Nature of the Study

The current study adopted the qualitative case study paradigm because it is a design that concentrates on understanding the individual perceptions and various qualitative opinions and perspectives about specific situations (Creswell, 2007). The major characteristic of case study design is its emphasis on "an intensive, holistic description and analysis of a single stance, phenomenon, or social unit" (Merriam, 1998, p. 21). For the purpose of this study, the case or unit of analysis under study was the perceptions of high school teachers of Arabic regarding developing cultural awareness of first-level Arabic language learners.

The study took place in two high schools within the same district in a large metropolitan Midwestern city. The city in which the two high schools are located is considered the catch pot of immigrants because it is an area where the concentration is largely Arab American (Merriam & Associates, 2002). Both high schools offer a sequence of eight levels of Arabic language instruction ranging from beginning to advanced. The first high school has three teachers of Arabic—other than the student researcher of this study—and the second high school has two.

This study utilized the qualitative case study research method through implementing one-on-one semi-structured in-depth interviews of five high school teachers of Arabic who teach or have taught first-level Arabic language classes within the same district. Since the investigation was designed to comprehend in depth how the case was explored by each informant, discovering that knowledge went through the inductive process, which is "the essence of discovery-oriented research" (Merriam & Associates, 2002, p. 121). All interviews were conducted in person by the researcher. The teachers' interviews were 20–30 minutes in length. Merriam and Associates (2002) explained that interviews "contain a mix of more and less structured questions" (p. 13). In this research, the interviews consisted of specific questions prepared in advance as well as questions that were not predetermined.

Each interview was tape recorded with two tape recorders to avoid lost data and to ensure accuracy and adequacy of recorded interviews. In addition, every interview was transcribed verbatim within 48 hours of the interview. The researcher utilized Seidel's (1998) qualitative method for organizing and analyzing data (teachers' semi-structured interviews) through studying the connection among the three parts: noticing things, collecting things, and thinking about things. The details of this approach are discussed in Chapter Three.

Research Questions

This study was driven by the following primary research question with two sub-questions:
- How do Arabic language teachers develop Arabic cultural awareness in first-level high school Arab language learners?
    1. What are Arabic language teachers' perceptions regarding the inclusion of cultural awareness in first-level Arabic language classes?
    2. What cultural activities do Arabic language teachers implement in an effort to generate cultural awareness in first-level Arab language classes?

Statement of Purpose

The purpose of this qualitative case study was to investigate Arab American high school teachers' perceptions regarding developing cultural awareness of first-level Arabic language learners. The aim of the study was to initiate a face-to-face conversation with teachers of Arabic about the concept of teaching the Arabic culture as it is integrated and incorporated in the Arabic language classroom. The researchers sought to understand the complexities and challenges that characterize Arabic cultural awareness, especially after the emergence of the new state graduation requirements for foreign language and the development of the Arabic National Standards in 2006. Listening to the voices of the teachers of Arabic was expected to help the researchers understand in depth the extent to which the Arabic program at the high school level is reaching its goals and learning outcomes (Fox & Diaz-Greenberg, 2006).

Conceptual Framework

The sociocultural theory developed by Lev Vygotsky (1978) served as the conceptual framework for this study. The central focus of this framework is that learning a language happens and develops through social and cultural interaction. Vygotsky's (1987) sociocultural theory is a quest for identifying two critical concepts of language learning: mediation and meaning. Mediation is "the process by which socially meaningful activities transform unmediated and natural behavior into higher mental processes through the use of tools" (Eun & Lim, 2009, p. 15). In other words, learning a language can take place in a sociocultural environment when learners create their own mediational tools or artifacts, such as picture images, picture cards, rehearsing, cooperation with one another, as well as adult guidance, and use them as aids in developing their linguistic abilities.

Vygotsky's (1978) sociocultural theory also concentrates on the learner's ability to endure meaningful communication and interactions with individuals in various social settings. In the context of Arabic language learning, purposeful social interaction among peers and between students and teachers is very significant and vital in the lives of the learners. Acknowledging that learning the Arabic language can happen through the "dynamic nature of the interplay between teachers, learners, and tasks" (Turuk, 2008, p. 248) is crucial for it creates a zone of proximal development (ZPD), where learners progress to a more advanced layer of understanding of the language as a result of this collective mediation.

Moreover, Vygotsky's emphasis on "interpersonal semiotic (verbal) interaction" (Eun & Lim, 2009, p. 22) is also in accord with the five Cs articulated in the standards of teaching Arabic as a world language. More specifically, the five Cs seek to integrate the learner's sociocultural experiences into classroom practice in order to mediate learning. This understanding of the cultural context of foreign language acquisition is fundamental because it is situated in the meaningful use of Arabic as the target language.

Furthermore, drawing on Vygotsky's sociocultural view of language learning, the five Cs invite learners and teachers of Arabic to reconceptualize language through meaningful interaction and dynamic conversations in the Arabic classroom. Equally important, the National Standards (2006) that were developed as a framework for foreign language learning and teaching asserted the notion that all language learning must be socially constructed because through contact with other people, learners are able to know "how, when, why, and to say what to whom" (p. 11).

Thus, within the sociocultural conceptual framework that the current study adopted, the researcher saw the five Cs—communication, cultures, connections, comparisons, and communities—as goals grounded in Vygotsky's (1978) perspective on learning and teaching Arab American high school students Arabic as a world language.

Definition of Terms

Arabic: A language spoken by 250 million people. It comprises both formal (*fusha*) and informal (*ammiyah*) varieties of the language (National Standards, 2006).

Arabs: People who speak Arabic, connect language and history, as well as share the same culture and heritage. Wingfield (2006) stated that Arabs are "a linguistic and cultural community, not a racial or religious group" (p. 253).

Attitude: For this study, *attitude* is the measure by which students and teachers of Arabic language are able to state their honest opinions and inclinations about how they perceive Arabic language instruction and the teaching of Arabic and culture (Bateman, 2008).

Cultural awareness: The ability to communicate with the rest of the world, as well as being able to understand and accept the negative and positive cultural traits that other people carry as much as we understand and accept our own. In other words, cultural awareness is the ability to value and evaluate the cultural practices, products, and perspectives of the culture studied (Schuetze, 2008).

Culture: What people constantly learn, acquire, and pass on to other people—acceptable and unacceptable patterns of behavior, traditions, religions, customs, and values—through verbal and nonverbal communication. In a workshop aimed at clarifying and examining the definition of culture, Bartoshesky (2003) pointed out that culture is sometimes split into the *explicit* aspects, such as foods, celebrations, and arts, and *implicit*, such as customs, traditions, and other social aspects. He also suggested integrating both types of cultures into world language instruction in order to help students study past and present historical events and movements with some sensitivity.

Foreign language: Also called *world language*; a term that has been used to reflect all languages acquired in schools except for the English language. Because of the remoteness of the term, foreign language educators were able to change it to a more diverse and global one.

Heritage language speakers: Depending on the amount of Arabic language and culture heard, spoken, or exposed to by speakers during childhood, heritage language speakers fall into three categories: those who can read and write fluently, those who come with lots of cultural knowledge but are not linguistically proficient at all, and those who have fair knowledge of the formal variety (MSA) but are quite proficient in their dialect (National Standards, 2006).

Less commonly taught languages: Languages such as Chinese, Arabic, Russian, Persian, and Korean are languages of the countries with whom the United States has economic ties, political and "strategic interest, and increasing cultural awareness" (National Standards, 2006, p. 18).

Modern standard Arabic (MSA): The language of the print, media, and newspapers.

Motivation: The tendency to participate and express desire in the study of a specific subject. In this study, *motivation* is the study of Arabic culture that enhances and increases the curiosity of Arab American learners in acquiring the language (Babler, 2006).

Perception: The way one conceives or becomes consciously aware of something via the five senses. It is the opinions of individuals based on personal experience, understanding, and environment.

Perspectives of culture: Attitudes, beliefs, and values of native language speakers of the language.

Practices of culture: Social communication and interaction among people.

Products of culture: Arts, music, literature, food, and games.

Sociocultural theory: A theory developed by Lev Vygotsky (1978), whose contention was that learning is an interactive experience in which learners collaborate with each other and interact in their ZPD. Vygotsky (1978) defined ZPD as the "distance between the actual developmental level as determined by independent problem solving and the level of potential development as determined through problem solving under adult guidance" (p. 86).

Socioeducational theory: A theory developed by Gardner (2001) that emphasizes the influence of students' intrinsic and extrinsic motivation on acquiring a foreign language, as well as on the students' attitudes toward the target language and culture and the role these attitudes play in being either highly motivated or not motivated to learn a foreign language (Gardner, 2001).

Target language: The terms *target language, foreign language,* and *world language* are used interchangeably in this study to describe the learning/teaching of Arabic as a foreign language.

Assumptions

Based on the existing literature on language and culture in world language classes and the new National Standards for foreign language, this researcher assumed that:
1. Arab American high school teachers teach or have taught first-level Arabic language classes in the same school district where the study took place.

2. High school teachers of Arabic have a clear understanding of the five Cs—communication, cultures, connections, comparisons, and communities—as well as of the three components of Arabic culture known as the three Ps—practices, products, and perspectives.
3. Arab American teachers of Arabic answered interview questions with the utmost honesty and truthfulness.
4. All five Arab American high school teachers of Arabic agreed to be interviewed.

Scope and Limitations

The purpose of this qualitative case study was to investigate Arab American high school teachers' perceptions regarding developing cultural awareness of first-level Arabic language learners. The research took place in two high schools within the same district. The study included face-to-face semi-structured in-depth interviews of five high school teachers of Arabic. However, the small number of teachers selected to be interviewed could be a limiting factor in generalizing results outside the school district where the study took place.

The research may have been limited in scope due to the fact the teachers who were selected to participate in the interviews at a later stage belonged to two high schools located in the metropolitan region only. This means that the results may not be generalized to other schools within or beyond the same school district. Finally, the teachers who participated in the study had a minimum of five years' experience in teaching Arabic at the high school level. This provided the researcher with a deeper understanding of the issues that were discussed when the interviews took place.

Delimitations

This study was delimited to investigating specific teaching issues relevant to Arab American teachers in two high schools within the same district. The study did not examine every educational challenge in the field of foreign language instruction. In addition, the study involved Arab American high school teachers who taught Arabic at the beginning level exclusively. Likewise, because the study was delimited to high school teachers, more research is needed to determine whether the findings of this current study could hold for other high school teachers from different contexts such as elementary or middle schools.

Significance of the Study

This study was designed to investigate Arab American high school teachers' perceptions regarding developing cultural awareness of first-level Arabic language learners. As more Arab American students enrolled in K–12 Arabic classes, there was a pressing need to address and meet Arab American high school students' cultural needs in the Arabic classroom. Thus, the study had the potential to locate specific areas where the Arabic curriculum was not reaching those needs in the Arabic classroom.

This topic is worth investigating because the Arabic community is expanding. Student enrollment in the K–12 Arabic program in the district are on the rise. Hence, strengthening and supporting the presence of Arabic as a heritage language in the schools extended the Arab American community's cultural identity. Ironically, the attacks of 9/11 and the continued discrimination against Arab Americans across the nation brought a sense of awareness to restore and protect the Arab American heritage and prestige through exposing their young to their own native language in their schools (Wingfield, 2006). This study may not only add to the repertoire of foreign language educators and teacher leaders but it may also encourage language researchers to conduct more research on Arab American elementary and middle school students in first-level Arabic language classes.

Positive Social Change

The aim of this research was to create positive social change in the lives of Arab American high school students and teachers of Arabic alike. The positive social change of this study could be noteworthy. This study is in response to the need of the Arab American community to validate its presence and preserve its roots by transmitting its cultural heritage to its children who are born in the United States. Sehlaoui (2008) asserted that "the loss of intergenerational language transmission is one of the most significant factors in language endangerment" (p. 287). Moreover, the study may prepare new generations of Arabic learners to join the growing international community socially, economically, and culturally.

Furthermore, the findings of this study may increase students' interest in learning Arabic not only as a world language but also as their heritage language. The study may also strengthen the social relations among Arab American students in the classroom and beyond the school setting when they are given the opportunity to appreciate and recognize the value of their own subcultures. Hence, despite the various cultural differences that exist among Arabs throughout the 22 Arab nations, there are some unique similarities and common features among those subcultures that could bring students together.

Understanding Arab American high school students' cultural needs may call for more effective teacher preparation and better instructional practices that reflect those needs in their classrooms. Additionally, the study could compel foreign language teachers to develop a real understanding of the standards for learning Arabic reflected in the five competencies: "Communication, Cultures, Connections, Comparisons, and Communities" (National Standards, 2006, p. 9).The inclusion of the Arabic culture in first-level Arabic language classes may require teachers to emphasize a sociocultural approach to language learning since "incorporating a social perspective of learners and language learning can make a significant contribution to furthering our understanding of the complexity of [the] second language learning process"(Swain & Deters, 2007, p. 820).

The results of this case study may suggest harmonizing the linguistic and cultural components of Arabic so that learning Arabic as a foreign language could take place with greater enthusiasm. Such harmony may be reached when the Arabic language classroom environment and Arabic curricula become purposeful, meaningful, and reflective of the students' linguistic and cultural needs. As in all foreign language learning, Arabic "learning and teaching is dialogic and all learning occurs in the social context of dialogue" (Sehlaoui, 2008, p. 290).

Conclusion

The surge in Arabic language enrollment among Arab American students in U.S. schools, especially after the tragic events of 9/11, called for the creation of the National Standards for foreign languages in 2006. The National Standards, Arabic being one, were generated from the premise that language and culture solidify the foundations of communication among individuals in this ever-changing world. The standards' primary goal was to align foreign language instruction with language curricula and empower foreign language students to be lifelong users of Arabic language and culture. However, the standards' emphasis on the concept of culture springs from the belief that "cultural values play a large role in the way different societies teach and learn in schools" (McLaren, 2007, p. 19). As a result, K–12 Arabic programs have experienced a shortage of highly qualified, certified, or even trained teachers of Arabic who are able to respond efficiently to that urgency. Native speakers of Arabic, often certified to teach in other fields, were hired to launch the Arabic programs without having the proper pedagogical training to teach Arabic as a foreign language.

The purpose of this qualitative case study was to understand in depth the individual perceptions of Arab American high school teachers of Arabic regarding developing cultural awareness of first-level Arabic language learners. Central to this study was the "urgent call for change with regard to the place of culture in the Arabic language curriculum" (Abdalla, 2006, p. 325). Vygotsky's (1978) sociocultural theory provided the conceptual framework for investigating and understanding how the students and teachers perceived the learning and teaching of Arabic within the social context in which the learning of the language took place. Ajayi (2008) argued, "Language is always used in relationship to the contexts and construal of contexts that are social and cultural" (p. 640). In other words, the social environment of the Arabic classroom could play a crucial role in learning the Arabic language.

Chapter Two provides a review of the pertinent literature related to the issue/unit of analysis under investigation. Chapter Three focuses on the methodology of the research. It describes the data that were collected and how the data were analyzed. Chapter Four presents the findings of the study resulting from the informants' past experiences through transcribed semi-structured interviews. Finally, Chapter Five summarizes and interprets the findings of this study. Recommendations and implications for possible extended future research conclude Chapter Five.

CHAPTER TWO
LITERATURE REVIEW

Introduction

Chapter Two investigates five interrelated key areas that support the study under investigation. It discusses the interrelatedness between language and culture. It also examines how language and culture are perceived in the field of foreign language learning, presents a summary of the standards for learning Arabic as a foreign language, and explains how culture is perceived in the National Standards by offering insight into specific ingredients of Arabic language education in order to strengthen and solidify its existence in the classrooms, as well as the need to incorporate the three Ps (practices, products, perspectives) of the Arabic culture into Arabic language curriculum. The last element draws on Vygotsky's sociocultural theory and Gardner's socioeducational theory as they established the cornerstone of the current qualitative case study.

Strategy for the Literature Review

The researcher's utilized multiple computer searches to build this literature review. The databases searched included Academic Search Premier, ProQuest Central, and Education Research Complete. However, Education Research Complete was the only database that offered a wealth of research studies on Arabic language and teaching and learning a foreign language. The Arabic language and culture component included the following key words and descriptors: *Arabic language and culture, Arabic as a world language, Arabic teaching in the United States, Arabic after 9/11, Arab Americans and Arabic as a heritage language, world languages and cultures, foreign language instruction, foreign language standards, practice in second language acquisition, learning a foreign language,* and *less commonly taught languages.* Moreover, in order to solidify the connection between past research and this current study, literature was searched on Vygotsky's sociocultural theory and Gardner's socioeducational theory. The key words and descriptors included *Arabic language and motivation, motivation and second language learning, mediation, sociocultural model, sociocultural framework, sociocultural theory, appropriateness and language learning, socioeducational theory, integrativeness and language learning, motivation and heritage language learners,* as well as *zone of proximal development.*

Historical Overview of the Interrelatedness of Language and Culture

The framework for teaching and learning culture relies heavily on demonstrating mastery and adequate knowledge about the nature of the target culture, developing appropriate behaviors in a specific linguistic and cultural setting, as well as discovering personal knowledge and self-awareness of values and attitudes. The integration of culture into the foreign language curriculum in general has suffered from a delayed start for many reasons. First, foreign language classes used to be conducted by utilizing the grammar–translation method (Mitchell & Vidal, 2001; Omaggio-Hadley, 2001), which concentrated on building a reading knowledge, grammar analysis, and translation from the students' first language to the target language (Ryding, 2006). The focus was also on the study of classical language (Latin and Greek) and literature of the language rather than the culture of those languages. Following the grammar–translation method, the direct method emerged. The direct method centered on the development of the learner's speaking skills through utilizing the use of pictures and profound literary figures but in a superficial way (Richards & Rodgers, 2001).

Seelye (1993) asserted that "learning a language in isolation of its cultural roots prevents one from becoming socialized into its contextual use" (p. 10). In other words, understanding the social meaning of certain words and expressions in a specific language is far more crucial than the ability to just read and write in the target language. He also offered six major goals to achieve if teachers intend to teach culture for understanding. The first goal is motivating foreign language learners and raising their interest and curiosity about learning the host culture. The second is helping language learners recognize that their ethnic background, social class, age, and gender can affect their linguistic and cultural behavior. The third is increasing learners' awareness of what cultural images are evoked when they come into contact with other people. The fourth goal is learning how to act and behave in normal and crisis situations in the target culture. This leads to the fifth goal, which emphasizes learners' understanding of why they act the way they do and how the cultural facets are interrelated. Finally, the sixth goal involves learners' ability to interpret and evaluate aspects of the target culture, such as media, literature, and other people's experiences.

The strong tie that connects language and culture was further enhanced by Taha (2006):

The linguistic meaning conveyed by the different utterances may, sometimes, add to or strengthen the overall meaning of the message, but, usually, it is the social meaning of words that clarif[ies] the cultural dimension of such utterances rather than their linguistic meaning. (p. 346)

The author elaborated by examining how native speakers of Arabic use the word *God—allah* in Arabic—not only in its religious context but also in sociocultural situations:

When someone looks at and admires something or someone else's beauty or act, we hear *allaah*.
When one is praising someone, we hear *alla-h-alla-h-allah*.
When one is caught red-handed doing things one should not do, we hear *allaaa-h-allaah*. (Taha, 2006, p. 357)

Similarly, Bollag (2008) stressed that after the 9/11 terrorist attacks, Americans were not aware of other cultures and what impact they could have in the United States. He further emphasized the need for a cultural literacy approach rather than just a language by using a more effective range of cultural expression. Similarly, Husseinali (2006) indicated that an Arab "cannot understand one's culture without knowing Arabic" (p. 395). In other words, one must not undervalue the connectedness between language and culture but rather view culture as an inseparable component of language (Abdalla, 2006).

Historically speaking, there have been three types of links between language education and culture instruction (Kramsch, 1985): universal, national, and local. As for universal links, Kramsch (1985) believed that when Latin and Hebrew were taught, universal understanding was reached through exploring literature, which allowed speakers of many diverse languages to interact and communicate socially beyond national boundaries. Later on, a sharp distinction between language and culture surfaced due to the rise of linguistic and literary criticism. Hence, the connectedness of language and literature was lost. That split between language teaching and culture teaching helped in creating a strictly grammatical language program, and culture became a fifth skill added to the listening, speaking, reading, and writing skills. As a result, language instruction became a social goal rather than a universal one especially for those who spoke and behaved according to the needs of the people and other acquaintances around them.

In an interesting study on the linguistic and cultural status of the Turkish and Moroccan communities in the Netherlands, where Dutch is spoken at home and at school, Extra and Yagmur (2010) documented that Turkish youngsters showed strong attachment to the Turkish language, whereas Moroccan youngsters strongly identified themselves with Islamic practices. The findings of the study suggested that "for Turkish youngsters, cultural self-awareness goes hand in hand with linguistic self-awareness" (Extra & Yagmur, 2010, p. 117). The researchers also reported stronger family ties for Turkish youngsters and a better grasp of literacy skills of the language than Moroccan youngsters, which in turn suggested that the latter would demonstrate more proficiency and mastery of the Dutch language than

Arabic. According to the researchers, the Moroccan youngsters showed "stronger sociocultural orientations toward the Dutch language and society than Turkish youngsters" (Extra &Yagmur, 2010, p. 124). The outcomes of the study suggested that both groups—Moroccan and Turkish—showed stronger feelings and affection toward their community languages—Arabic and Turkish—than to Dutch, even though Dutch was the language they had chosen for interaction. In addition, the researchers noted that the only difference seen between the Turkish and the Moroccan youngsters in terms of their sociocultural inclinations was the degree of self-identification. While both groups identified themselves as either Moroccan-Dutch or Turkish-Dutch, the number of Turkish participants who labeled themselves as Turkish only was much higher than the Moroccans who labeled themselves as Moroccan only.

Arabic Language Teaching in the United States

The Arab world consists of 22 countries, including Palestine who are brought together by a common linguistic and cultural heritage. The first Arabs who immigrated to the United States, particularly to Metropolitan Detroit, were Syrian/Lebanese Christians, in an attempt to seek employment at the auto factories that Henry Ford had established. That migration was followed by Yemenis, other Lebanese immigrants from the south of Lebanon, as a result of the civil war, followed by Iraqi Chaldeans, whose language is modern Aramaic—the language of Jesus. Following the Gulf War, Metropolitan Detroit also welcomed a huge number of Iraqi refugees mainly from the northern and southern parts of Iraq. Also, a bulk of Arab Americans from Palestine immigrated to the United States after the 1948 and 1967 Arab-Israeli wars. The exact population of Arab Americans in Metropolitan Detroit remains unknown; however, according to the Arab American Institute Foundation (2010), the estimates range from 409,000 to 490,000.

The field of teaching Arabic as a foreign language has undergone many important changes in the past several decades. The first stage began in the mid-seventeenth century when Arabic was initiated at Harvard University between 1654 and 1672, followed by Yale University and Princeton Theological Seminary (Ryding, 2006). The second stage started in 1967 when the Center for Arabic Study Abroad (CASA) was established by the University of California at Berkeley and Los Angeles, University of Chicago, and University of Michigan, among others (Belnap, 2006). The CASA program was constructed as a study-abroad Arabic program in the United States and Cairo. Belnap (2006) stated that "one significant advantage of this model is that a small institution could hire one Arabic faculty member and mount a program that would produce students with advance-and Super-level Arabic proficiency" (p. 177) because it relies heavily on teaching both MSA and Egyptian dialect, in order to produce culturally proficient Arabic learners.

In the late 1990s, a unique Arabic program was initiated between the Fez program in Morocco and Washington University in St. Louis, Missouri, in addition to teaching a variety of intensive courses in both MSA and colloquial Arabic at the

University of Wisconsin-Madison in 2004 (Abdalla, 2006). Moreover, according to Sehlaoui (2008), the Arabic language "was introduced to the United States as early as the 1880s, when Arab immigrants began arriving in the country in considerable numbers" (p. 280). She reported that the number of native-born Americans who speak Arabic as their first language in America is over 3 million. Hence, preserving the Arabic language, traditions, history, and cultural heritage was, and still is, a big concern for the Arab community. As a result, "Arab American families resorted to private schools or weekend programs to preserve the language" (Sehlaoui, 2008, p. 280) among their own children who were born in the United States. In fact, the National Capital Language Resource Center (2006) reported that Arabic is taught in approximately 110 private and charter schools across the nation. In support of maintaining heritage languages, J. S. Lee (2005) emphasized that "our nation needs to look more closely at how we can creatively and strategically tap into the heritage language communities to promote intergenerational transmission of heritage languages" (p. 254).

Teaching Arabic as a foreign language did not draw much attention from federal and local governments before the 2001 terrorist attacks (Al-Batal, 2007; Al-Batal & Belnap, 2006; Allen, 2007; Bollag, 2008; A. V. Brown, 2009; National Standards, 2006; Sehlaoui, 2008; Taha, 2006). However, the growth in interest in the teaching and learning of Arabic language and culture brought with it numerous problems, issues, and challenges. According to Allen (2007), the Arabic teaching profession had to face the problems of finding qualified and competent teachers of Arabic who were residents in the United States, creating and developing materials that could meet the needs of advanced learners of Arabic, and enhancing study-abroad opportunities for learners who were interested in becoming more proficient in the language.

Likewise, Al-Batal and Belnap (2006) explained that some of the daunting challenges the Arabic teaching profession was facing emerged because of "long years of neglect and the absence of a national agenda for foreign language education in the United States" (p. 269). Those challenges, he believed, stemmed from the rapid establishment of new Arabic programs at colleges and universities, the growing number of students enrolled in Arabic summer programs across the nation as well as abroad, and the lack of the inability to identify highly qualified teachers of Arabic as a foreign language.

In addition, the teaching of Arabic as a foreign language has created persistent disagreement among teachers of Arabic on whether K–12 language learners should be taught MSA—the language of the newspapers and speeches—or a dialect, or a combination of both (National Standards, 2006). During the 1960s and 1970s, the next essential teaching methodology that emerged mainly from behavioral psychology was the audio-lingual method (ALM; Abdalla, 2006). The goal of ALM was to concentrate on learners' **oral comprehension of their daily activities in the** target language, which in turn would require some level of sociocultural and sociolinguistic awareness and appropriateness. As a result, the grammar–translation method and ALM became very popular in the field of teaching Arabic as a foreign language. In fact, both methods were widely used in several Arabic programs.

However, there was a great need to find better teaching approaches that could positively impact the teaching and learning of Arabic language and culture. Finding more effective teaching and learning methodologies was critical due "to the diglossia nature of the Arabic language and its complex grammatical and derivational system" (Abdalla, 2006, p. 319). Sawaie (2006) defined *diglossia* as "the existence of two speech varieties in the same language, each of which is simultaneously used in specialized domains in a linguistic community" (p. 372). In the case of Arabic, there is MSA, used by educated Arabic speakers in formal situations such as documentaries, speeches, and news broadcasts. On the other hand, regional and local dialectical varieties are used when communicating with other people on a daily basis (Van Mol, 2006). MSA, as Al-Bataland Belnap (2006) assured, "is not a language of conversation [but rather] a language of intellectual exchange" (p. 396). Speakers of Arabic usually mix both as they speak. The fact is that the Arab world consists of 22 Arabic countries, which in turn contain numerous spoken Arabic dialects. That makes it impossible for teachers to choose one Arabic dialect to teach; therefore, teaching spoken Arabic remained a course taught over MSA. According to Axelon (2006), the State Department ranked Arabic as a Category 4 language because of its "right-to-left cursive script, varied dialects and pronunciation unfamiliar to westerners" (p. 43), which in turn calls for the urgent need to introduce Arabic to learners at a younger age.

The 1990s witnessed the emergence and implementation of a new approach to foreign language learning. That approach was the communicative approach or communicative language learning, which emphasizes the need to incorporate the four language skills—speaking, listening, reading, and writing—alongside the cultural skill (Abdalla, 2006). Swaffar (2006) also thought of communicative competence as a trend that "could take on an entirely new meaning if the ability to read, write, listen, reflect, and communicate intelligently about a culture's multiple facets were to become the chief goal of foreign language programs at all levels" (p. 249). That innovative practice had a positive impact not only on the teaching and learning of Arabic but also on the whole field of learning and teaching Arabic as a foreign language. Teachers of Arabic became facilitators rather than lecturers, and oral or written authentic materials were very much integrated. Despite the diglossia, the communicative approach is still very much supported and widely adopted because it helps students practice real conversations about real social situations, such as telephone conversations, buying and selling in the market, booking flights, and asking for directions, which are usually conducted in spoken Arabic.

In addition, Kramsch (2006) stated that the notion of communicative competence was introduced as a "reaction against an audio-lingual instructional approach often referred to as 'drill and kill'" (p. 249). However, Schulz (2006) emphasized that communicative competence was never a sufficient goal in foreign language contexts because "neither time nor instructional context is sufficient or appropriate to develop a meaningful lasting level of proficiency" (p. 253). Still, the scholar did not support the return of the grammar-translation model; instead, she proposed that foreign language teachers reflect and reexamine their instructional practices in their language classrooms so that language learners gain insight into "how language reflects culture, how culture reflects language and language use and the language learning process and strategies useful for language learning" (Schulz, 2006, p. 254).

The Standards for Learning Arabic as a Foreign Language: A New Road Map

In developing the standards for learning Arabic as a foreign language, the 11 committee members, known as the Task Force, represented by teachers, administrators, researchers, and scholars, had to resolve issues related to the role of culture in the Arab world. The National Standards (2006) stated that although Arabic is spoken by more than 250 million people, each of the 22 Arab countries has its own unique culture; "however, there are highly recognizable societal features that make up what can generally be called Arab culture" (p. 117), such as Arab family relationships. For this reason, the Task Force chose to approach the Arab culture as a whole.

The turn of the twenty-first century has witnessed incredible change in the teaching and learning of foreign languages across the nation, especially when the National Standards for the teaching of foreign languages were developed and required to be incorporated into foreign language classrooms. The National Standards emerged in order to "provide an opportunity to create a skeleton or a rough idea of what some of the essential skills in knowledge in a given field have to offer" (Riley, Abu-Saad, & Hermes, 2005, p. 187).

However, Wilbur (2007) believed that foreign language standards were basically based on theory, because foreign language teachers can have "an understanding of the standards without fully understand[ing] how to practically integrate them into curriculum planning, instruction, and assessment" (p. 87). Thus, the standards for learning Arabic as a foreign language were developed mainly to "enable teachers and administrators in grades K-12 to give their students an effective working knowledge of the Arabic language and Arab culture" (National Standards, 2006, p. 118).

Even though the standards for foreign language learning were affiliated with the following five interconnected goals—communication, cultures, connections, comparisons, and communities—each learning-specific standard was explained and examined as a separate entity to reflect the various syntactic and cultural differences among foreign languages.

Figure 2.1. The Five Cs of Foreign Language Study

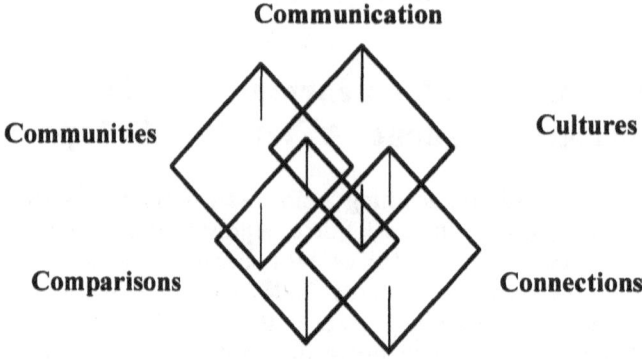

Specifically, the standard of *communication* for learning Arabic focuses on students' ability to converse appropriately in various formal and informal contexts. The ultimate goal of this standard is to help students "present information, concepts, and ideas to an audience of listeners or readers on a variety of topics" (National Standards, 2006, p. 122).

Equally important, the standard of *cultures* for learning Arabic emphasizes students' understanding "of the relationship between the practices and perspectives of the various cultures of the Arab world" (National Standards, 2006, p. 128). In other words, students will demonstrate familiarity of the cultural practices needed to interact and socialize with other people who belong to various Arabic countries. Moreover, the standard of *cultures* examines students' ability to "demonstrate an understanding of the relationship between the products and perspectives of the various cultures of the Arab world" (National Standards, 2006, p. 130). Thus, there is great emphasis on cultural appreciation of the traditions, customs, and values that the Arab culture reflects.

Furthermore, the third standard for learning Arabic, *connections*, focuses on students' ability to use Arabic in order to "connect with other disciplines, acquire information, and recognize viewpoints that are only available through the Arabic language and culture" (National Standards, 2006, pp. 133–134). Hence, the more students can relate the knowledge they receive in other content area classes to their learning of the Arabic language and culture in their Arabic classes, the better they are able to refine their communication with other proficient speakers of Arabic.

In addition, Arabic language learners may gain awareness of the linguistic and cultural nature of their own language as they progress in the study of Arabic language culture. Thus, it is through the standard of *comparisons* where Arabic language learners are able to "demonstrate understanding of the nature of language through comparisons between Arabic and their own language and the cultures of the Arab world and their own" (National Standards, 2006, pp. 137–138). This means that students can expand and enrich their cultural knowledge through learning the Arabic language. The standard also encourages learners to discover other people's practices, products, and perspectives that are the same or different from their own. Hence, by discovering how to encode certain expressions and words linguistically, and by giving extra attention to how those words are appropriately expressed in cultural settings, learners of Arabic may be able to view the rest of the world with more gratitude (National Standards, 2006).

The last standard for learning Arabic is *communities*. This goal emphasizes that students "show evidence of becoming lifelong learners by using Arabic for personal enjoyment and enrichment" (National Standards, 2006, pp. 141–142). The standard also indicates that when students reach a point where they become intrinsically motivated to continue learning and mastering the Arabic language, they will seek out contexts beyond the school setting in order to further their linguistic and cultural competency.

The National Standards (2006) also include benchmarks known as Sample Progress Indicators, which contain samples necessary to help teachers develop learning scenarios for the sake of meeting the needs of their students. Certainly, the standards are not meant to be the curriculum but rather a

> Road map [whose] ultimate objective is to assert the belief that all students can develop competency in the Arabic language and appreciation for Arabic culture; that all students can learn, and instruction must be interactive, learner-centered, and reflect best practices. (National Standards, 2006, p. 118)

Arabic Culture in the National Standards for Foreign Language Learning

The National Standards (2006) confirmed that "knowledge of the cultural context in which languages are spoken is essential to achieving true mastery of a foreign language" (p. 31). Hence, the *cultures* goal consists of two standards. The first focuses on the practices of the target culture studied (2.1), whereas the second (2.2) emphasizes the products associated with the perspectives of the host culture.

- Standard 2.1: "Students demonstrate an understanding of the relationship between the practices and the perspectives of the various cultures of the Arab world" (National Standards, 2006, p. 128).
- Standard 2.2: "Students demonstrate an understanding of the relationship between the products and perspectives of the various cultures of the Arab world" (National Standards, 2006, p. 51).

In the first standard, learners of Arabic as a foreign language develop their cultural awareness by identifying and interpreting the social interactions and diversity of cultural attitudes, customs, traditions, and beliefs of native speakers of Arabic. The second standard emphasizes cultural appreciation, where learners of Arabic as a foreign language recognize and interpret various cultural products, such as literature, science, medicine, film, calligraphy, and architecture. Nevertheless, the emphasis on Arabic culture is also evident in the standards of *connections* (3.2) *and comparisons* (4.2):

- Standard 3.2: "Students acquire information and recognize viewpoints that are only available through the Arabic language and culture" (National Standards, 2006, p. 134).
- Standard 4.2: "Students demonstrate understanding of the concept of culture through comparisons between the cultures of the Arab world and their own" (National Standards, 2006, p. 138).

In Standard 3.2, learners of Arabic as a foreign language broaden their understanding of the Arabic culture through using multiple Arabic resources, such as media types, online newspapers and magazines, as well as cultural events. In Standard 4.2, learners of Arabic expand their understanding and appreciation of Arabic culture through comparing and contrasting the practices, products, and perspectives of their own culture and those associated with the Arabic culture.

In an article on the significance of teaching culture in foreign language classrooms and the multiple meaning that the term *culture* embodies, Tang (2006) presented three parts of culture: achievement, informational, and behavioral, along with the three components of culture, the three Ps—practices, products, and perspectives—that were advocated by the National Standards. He indicated that even though learning the products (foods and music) and practices (patterns of social interaction) of a new language is basic in acquiring a foreign language, "the perspectives of the target culture are what teachers ought to concentrate on in foreign language instruction" (Tang, 2006, p. 86). This is important but very challenging on the part of the foreign language teacher due to the difficulty in explaining intangible things such as values and attitudes of people. In fact, "the products and practices are derived from the philosophical perspectives that form the world view of a cultural group" (National Standards, 2006, p. 47; Figure 2.2).

Figure 2.2 The Interdependence of the Three Ps

Perspectives
Meanings, Attitudes,
Values, Ideas

Practices
Patterns of
Social Interactions

Products
Books, Food,
Tools, Music Games

Similarly, in an article that examined the role of culture in foreign language classroom settings, Fox and Diaz-Greenberg (2006) stated that demonstrating an understanding of the practices, products, and perspectives of the culture studied would help language learners reach a deeper level of understanding because "cultural understanding extends beyond an individual's ability to state facts or know about a country's cultural celebrations to being able to engage in culturally relevant and sensitive dialogue" (p. 405).

In her book on culture and education, Nieto (2008) explained that "the term culture can mean different things to different people in different contexts" (p. 128). Culture, for example, can pertain to what sophisticated and elite people may do in their leisure time, or it can reflect the customs, traditions, holidays, celebrations, and values carried by a group of people. However, according to Nieto (2008), culture needs to be related to learning but cannot be reduced to just food and holidays because culture is dynamic, always changing due to political and social conditions; multifaceted, influenced by location, language use, and social or educational level; as well as socially constructed and promoted. Similarly, Merriman and Nicoletti (2008) emphasized that teachers of a foreign language must go beyond teaching traditional forms of culture, such as food festivals and holidays, and focus more "on global diversity and its effects on current and future American culture" (p. 18), simply because foreign language acquisition has become empowered and driven by learning the culture of the speakers of the target language.

Theories of Language Acquisition

In the last two centuries, there have been various movements and exploration of foreign language teaching in the United States. Considerable interest has been given to the significance of teaching culture in order to master the target language. Despite the fact that one of the theories prioritizes itself over the other, there exist few distinguished theories for understanding the value of foreign language acquisition. For the purpose of this study, Vygotsky's (1929, 1978) sociocultural theory and Gardner's (1985, 2001, 2006) socioeducational theory were explored.

Vygotsky and Sociocultural Theory

Sociocultural theory, led by Vygotsky (1929, 1978), asserted that social interaction is essential to the individual's cognitive, social, and cultural development. From the sociocultural perspective, the process of learning is influenced by community and culture. This relevance to social factors is not a superficial one; language cannot grow and flourish except through real social means of communication among peers. Individuals, as Toohey (2006) asserted, "are always socially and culturally situated as they struggle to make meaning of text" (p. 279). Vygotsky (1929) believed that learners' capability to communicate in more than one language will help them see the connection between their own native language and culture and the target language and culture they are learning. In other words, knowledge of other people's linguistic and cultural rituals leads to appreciation of one's own language and culture as well.

Moreover, the social context of learning is essential for cognitive growth and development. Vygotsky (1986) distinguished between language and thought. He emphasized that thought grows when language is developed. In other words, thought is believed to be biologically developed, whereas language is the product of social interaction among social groups. According to Vygotsky (as cited in Turuk, 2008), sociocultural theory advocates that children learn primarily through interactions, contact, and communication with people as the first step (inter-psychological plane), then add their personal value to that knowledge they acquire (intrapsychological plane). Sociocultural theory emphasizes the significance of having a learning situation that acknowledges "the dynamic nature of the interplay between teachers, learners, and tasks, and provide[s] a view of learning as arising from interaction with others" (Turuk, 2008, p. 247). Vygotsky (1978) differentiated between *intramental* and *intermental* psychological abilities:

> Every function in the child's cultural development appears twice: first, on the social level and later on the individual level; first, between people (inter-psychological), and then inside the child (intrapsychological). This applies equally to voluntary attention, to logical memory, and to the formulation of concepts. All the higher functions originate as actual relations between human individuals. (p. 57)

Nevertheless, one of Vygotsky's greatest contributions of the sociocultural theory to the field of education was the concept of ZPD. Vygotsky (1978) defined ZPD as "a construct that refers to those functions that have not yet matured but are in the process of maturation" (p. 86). In other words, acquiring a new language is incremental; it takes time, patience, and effort to master or be proficient in another language. However, in a sociocultural classroom, learning must be interactive, communicative, functional, and, of course, cultural. Turuk (2008) explained that it was Vygotsky's belief that:

> The established assessment tools and tests delivered to students only measure the learners' overall level of development of the language but do not reflect the learners' actual performance and ability; therefore, the study of ZPD was crucial because it is the dynamic region of sensitivity in which the transition from inter-psychological to intra-psychological function takes place. (p. 248)

In the context of schools, foreign language teachers must find and create effective means to help language learners progress in their acquisition of the target language. Language, as Thomas (2005) asserted, "mediates between cognition and social experience; that the difference between an individual's present and potential capacities can be accessed within a zone of proximal development" (p. 297).

Sociocultural theory emphasizes two concepts: mediation and scaffolding. According to Vygotsky (1978), mediation is central to learning because it does not take place in isolation for it is enhanced and shaped by other people's learning experiences as they interact with one another. Learners move from one level of knowledge to another through social interaction with one another by using one of the most important tools: language. Hence, it is this process of appropriation that brings learning of the host language to the surface.

In the sociocultural theory of Vygotsky (1978), the notions of meaning of mediation are the most critical issues impacting students' learning of a second/foreign language. The sociocultural perspective emphasizes "the integrated nature of individual (psychological) and social (environmental) elements on the learning process" (Eun & Lim, 2009, p. 14). It also indicates that in the context of foreign language instruction and through the notion of mediation, language learners go through three mediational means: (a) mediation through material artifacts such as using picture cards to mediate their remembering process, (b) mediation through symbolic systems such as rehearsing the new vocabulary words, and (c) mediation through other adults who may have a direct influence on the learners' lives.

In addition, the Vygotskian perspective understands the concept of meaning as one that allows real social and dynamic interaction between adults and children to take place in order to facilitate social and linguistic development. Hence, the developmental process is always "initiated between people (the intermental plane) and only gradually moves into the individuals' psychological plane (Eun & Lim, 2009, p. 17).

Similarly, the concept of scaffolding in the classroom setting emphasizes the need to model the task, skill, and strategy to be delivered before shifting responsibility fully to learners. Scaffolding is a performance that demands certain assistance and unlimited guidance from the teacher before he or she dismantles the scaffold.

Significance of Sociocultural Theory on Foreign Language Teaching

In foreign language contexts, sociocultural theory emphasizes the social use of language and the meaningful interaction among language learners in the classroom. It also advocates that acquiring a language be dynamic, for overemphasis on teaching facts, rote memorization, grammar, as well as "fixed routine and dogmatic treatment of skills" (Turuk, 2008, p. 254) only hinder learners' cognitive abilities to construct meaning and demotivate them to learn the language. Thus, determining the learners' ZPD is crucial to language learning and acquisition because it helps language teachers acknowledge what their students are able to accomplish on their own and what they need coaching in to achieve.

In an article that examined how university teachers were able to help teacher candidates of various cultural backgrounds understand how sociocultural factors influence schooling altogether, K. Brown and Kraehe (2010) explained that the students were engaged in various activities that included whole-class minilessons, group discussions, collaborative video projects, along with film cases, where gender and race played a crucial role in bringing those students to one another and in connecting with the film. The authors stated that "Arab[s] and Arab Americans make up another racial/ethnic minority group in the United States [that] until the events of 9/11, seldom have been addressed in the literature on sociocultural influences on schooling" (K. Brown & Kraehe, 2010, p. 104). The researchers also provided their students with a video case of an Arab American girl whose teacher failed to see her cultural background as a positive thing, by not allowing her to interact and communicate with any of her peers in class. Through that one sociocultural influence, the study highlighted how students'"understanding about sociocultural knowledge can shift and become more complex in a single course when provided scaffolded learning opportunities to develop more complex understanding about the role sociocultural factors play in the schooling process" (K. Brown & Kraehe, 2010, p. 105).

In another study that investigated sociocultural background variables, such as cultural identification, cultural participation, and use of Spanish beyond school setting, Oh and Au (2005) indicated that the process of losing heritage languages in general is on the rise and accelerating due to the fact that "heritage languages now more often [are] lost during the 2nd generation" (p. 229). However, the study was launched to better understand what might trigger heritage language learners' interest in relearning the Spanish language in adulthood. The findings offered preliminary evidence that giving heritage language learners ample opportunities to participate in various cultural activities in and beyond the school setting and using Spanish in many learning contexts was key to successfully achieve mastery of their language.

Moreover, in a study aimed at understanding the pedagogic value of children's learning by endorsing sociocultural theory in the classroom, Black (2007) argued that all learning must be student-centered and all teaching must be interactive and "operating in socially mediated practices" (p. 274). Hence, language can be acquired and successfully transmitted when student–student and student–teacher contact time is maximized through the use of language.

Furthermore, Vygotsky stated that heritage languages are usually developed and enriched from "below to above, [whereas] the development of the foreign language moves from above to below" (as cited in J. Yi & Kellogg, 2006, p. 38). For Vygotsky, foreign languages ought to be approached and delivered the same way mother tongue languages or first languages are taught. He truly believed that learning a foreign language "raises the level of the child's native speech in much the same way that learning algebra raises the level of his arithmetic thinking" (Vygotsky, 1987, p. 180). Hence, language learners could reach higher levels of knowledge when they exercise control over spelling, pronunciation, and definition of words. That level can be attained and supported by the presence of the notion of mediation by others and by the act of ZPD.

In a sociocultural approach to second/foreign language acquisition and learning, RosiSolé (2007) interviewed 20 language learners at the university level in an attempt to understand how they create their own identities—what cultural values and social realities they have carried as they have acquired the target language. For the researcher, language is not only a means of communication but is also "the place where identity is constructed, as it is the language [in which] we organize our social selves" (RosiSolé, 2007, p. 205). In other words, language learners cannot possibly develop new linguistic skills without feeling affiliated with the new language and community. The importance of belonging to the target language community cannot be underestimated or ignored because it is through "a real dialogue with the listener that the learner can negotiate the self and adopt new roles and identities" (RosiSolé, 2007, p. 206).

Drawing on the sociocultural theoretical perspective on the relationship between literacy and identity, Bartlett (2005) argued that literacy instruction must be supported by interaction among groups and attained through acquisition or informal instruction rather than through formal or overt instruction. He added that cultural artifacts promote new selves, identities, and social awareness, as well as empower learners' social relations. From the Vygotskian notion of semiotic mediation, artifacts such as poetry, drama, narrative, journal writing, and cartoons trigger human modification of actions, feelings, and cognition because the notion of mediation is "more than a means for solving problems and creating learning possibilities" (Thorne, 2005, p. 399).

According to McConachy (2009), language teachers can heighten their "awareness of elements of sociocultural context and also develop analytical questions for learners" (p. 116) by devising various methods to ensure that language learners perceive communicative competence as a concept that stems from real interaction/communication between people rather than just finding information and answering questions in a dialogue. Moreover, language teachers can raise their students' sociocultural awareness by teaching them skills of analyzing and interpreting language use rather than locating information in a passage that is irrelevant to their lives. Comparative questions, for instance, are great learning devices in foreign language classrooms for they encourage students to compare "an aspect of interaction or sociocultural relationship noticed in the dialogue/s they are using with that of their native culture" (McConachy, 2009, p. 122). This takes one back to the standard of *comparisons* stated in the National Standards for learning foreign languages. Thus, dialogues that reflect students' real lives enhance their communicative competence, and the skills they learn when involved in interpreting, reflecting, and analyzing language use are what the sociocultural theory advocates.

Thus, sociocultural theory, once labeled by Lantolf and Thorneas "cultural-historical psychology" (as cited in De la O LópezAbeledo, 2008, p. 178), asserts that individuals cannot be isolated from their surroundings, community, and social contexts. Language learners are influenced by the cultural and social milieu in which they interact. The Vygotskian sociocultural model emphasizes the importance of understanding the individual's self-being through understanding how that individual is socially and culturally situated and how the language he or she uses is practiced. Hence, understanding the individual's self-being is critical because it is not isolated from his or her identity (Vygotsky, 1978).

Gardner and Socioeducational Theory

Foreign language instruction must have its curriculum aligned with the standards and benchmarks mandated by the state. Hence, this researcher's intent was to help students communicate in Arabic, develop deeper understanding of their own culture, connect that with other content areas, compare and contrast their own culture with the acquired one, as well as become lifelong learners capable of taking their language and culture beyond the school setting. This perspective leads to the discussion of the critical role that motivation has on learning Arabic or any foreign language.

Influence of Motivation on Acquiring a World Language

Understanding the relationship between intrinsic motivation, where accomplishments are reached through personal choices for their own sake, and extrinsic motivation, where goals are sought for external rewards (Gardner, 2001), is essential in the context of language acquisition. Language learners who are highly motivated to learn a second language can reach proficiency in the target language because they enjoy the learning process and strive for language and cultural competency with enthusiasm (Gardner, 1985).

Motivation to learn a language requires that the learner have a persistent attempt for the effort to learn the language, the desire to achieve success, as well as the enthusiasm or the positive affect so he or she can enjoy the learning (Gardner, 1985). As an affective construct, the socioeducational model assumes that language learners must exhibit all three attributes combined—desire, effort, and positive affect—because they adequately assume motivation. Lacking the desire to learn a language would impede the learner's overall language performance; "the relationship between positive attitudes and L2 [second language] investment/ motivation can be influenced significantly by learners' amount of contact in/between the two cultures" (Xingsong, 2006, p. 12). Equally important, the learner's willingness to excel in another language only alleviates his or her language anxiety.

According to Gardner (2006), the socioeducational model of language acquisition carries five assumptions. The first assumes that learning a language requires a level of competence that allows learners to communicate and interact with other speakers of the target language. The second assumption is centered on the process of learning a language in association with the learners' abilities and motivation—two individual, different characteristics—that influence language learning. The third assumption emphasizes that the individual differences in motivation can be the result of one's cultural, social, educational, as well as personal experiences. The fourth assumption acknowledges that learning a language takes place in formal and informal contexts. Gardner (2006) stated that formal contexts are those in which "there is specific training in the language" (p. 240), such as the language classroom, whereas informal contexts are "those providing opportunities to use and experience the language such as social settings" (p. 240). The last assumption indicates that both formal and informal language learning contexts will result in linguistic outcomes that involve general knowledge about the language and nonlinguistic outcomes, which involves the learners' language attitude, motivation, desire to interact with other speakers, self-determination, as well as language anxiety (Gardner, 2006). A schematic representation of the socioeducational model is presented in Figure 2.3.

Figure 2.3. The Socioeducational Model

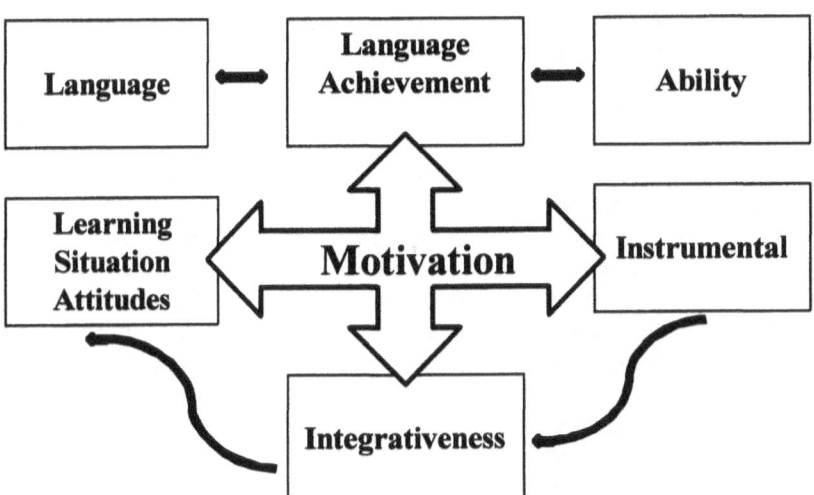

According to Figure 2.3, language attitude falls under two categories: integrativeness and attitudes. Integrativeness is understood as learners' wanting to adopt behavioral aspects that are usually associated with the host language and is measured by attitudes toward the people who belong to the target language, whereas attitudes are closely connected with learners' motivation, language anxiety, and learning strategies. Moreover, language acquisition may take place in formal or informal language learning environments. In the formal language learning environment, motivation, language anxiety, intelligence, and learning strategies play a major role in learners' acquisition of the target language. On the other hand, in the informal language learning environment, motivation is the most critical.

In addition, language learning consists of two outcomes: linguistic outcomes and nonlinguistic outcomes. For the purpose of this study, *linguistic outcomes* refer to learners' mastery of the syntax, grammatical structure, morphology, and phenomenology of the Arabic language, whereas *nonlinguistic outcomes* refer to the affective part of learning Arabic as a foreign language, such as attitudes and values. Gardner's (1985) socioeducational model postulated that enduring the link between the linguistic and nonlinguistic outcomes would influence learners' overall proficiency of a second/foreign language and culture. In other words, students learning Arabic as a foreign language must possess the ability and motivation to learn the language because both are linked to language achievement. In addition, the socioeducational model would indicate that language learners with high levels of integrativeness would consider the Arabic language learning situation a positive experience.

The figure also indicates a close link between attitudes toward the learning situation and integrativeness to motivation, which in turn means that "levels of motivation are influenced and maintained by *Attitudes* toward the *Learning Situation* and *Integrativeness*" (Gardner, 2006, p. 245).Finally, the socioeducational model may indicate that Arab American students who are not truly highly motivated to learn the Arabic language and culture may experience aroused levels of anxiety. Hence, motivation is perceived as a remarkably complex but dynamic ingredient for it involves "the reasons why we want to learn, the strength of our desire to learn, the kind of person we are, and the task and our estimation of what it requires of us" (McDonough, 2007, p. 369).

Furthermore, Gardner and Lambert (1959) proposed two types of purposes: integrative motive and instrumental motive. *Integrative motive* refers to the learner's willingness to communicate and interact with people of the host language culture, whereas *instrumental motive* refers to the learner's desire to learn a foreign language and culture. In the current study, learning Arabic language and culture can be both integrative and instrumental. It is Arabic learners' initial motive for studying Arabic language and culture that determines to what extent they will be able to achieve the goal of learning Arabic and better understanding and perhaps appreciating Arabic culture.

In a study that examined the relationship between foreign language motivation and self-efficacy, Pei-Hsuan (2008) determined that students who were highly motivated to learn the foreign language they were taking and "those who did not experience anxiety in the foreign language classroom were more apt to experience academic success in Spanish, German, and French" (p. 86). It was also suggested that foreign language teachers can help their students set realistic goals by giving them honest feedback and utilizing multiple teaching methods to alleviate anxiety and optimize the learning experience.

Similarly, in a Japanese classroom research on motivational strategy use in the English as a foreign language (EFL) context, Sugita and Takeuchio (2010) investigated 15 motivational techniques and teaching methods utilized by foreign language teachers in order to promote and endure language learning. The researchers defined motivational strategies as "techniques consciously used by EFL teachers as ways to promote language-learning motivation" (p. 24). The study concluded that the effectiveness of various teaching methods used by teachers in the EFL context varies according to the learners' proficiency level of English. It also resulted in highlighting four major motivational strategies that were linked to learners' motivation: foreign language teachers' assessment and measurement tools that go beyond pencil-and-paper tests, teachers' willingness to share with their students their own personal interest in the foreign language they are teaching, teachers' continuous regular feedback of the learners' work, as well as teachers' acceptance of the fact that their students will continue to make mistakes as they grow linguistically and culturally.

In another research study that investigated perceptions on language learning strategy use by Arabic-speaking females learning EFL, Riazi (2007) acknowledged that successful language learners are those who use "a wide range of effective language learning strategies in a systematic and organized way" (p. 43). This implies that language learners can improve their learning of the target language through proper strategy training, which in turn can be enhanced by their foreign language teachers who can allocate enough class time in order to discuss and explain the language strategy. Thus, it is important to give language learners the opportunity to share the responsibility for their language learning so they "learn how to compensate for the deficiency in their second language proficiency" (Riazi, 2007, p. 440).

In a study that examined two aspects of motivation—the students' language choices and the learning effort exerted in learning a foreign language—Csizér and Dörnyei (2005) concluded that foreign language learners who are "in a learning environment that does not offer extensive opportunities for direct contact with L2 speakers, the main source of contact with the language will be indirect, through exposure to various L2 specific cultural products" (p. 29). The researchers defined motivation as a "concept that explains why people behave as they do rather than how successful their behavior will be" (Csizér & Dörnyei, 2005, p. 20). In fact, language learners' abilities to learn a foreign language can be another factor, other than motivation, that may affect the learning of a foreign language. For the purpose of this study, that could mean that the extent of the Arab American high school students' confidence in acquiring the Arabic language will determine their interest in learning and engaging with their cultural products as they advance.

Thus, language learners can achieve high levels of competence in the target language only if they choose to stay in the language programs beyond the required year-long classes. According to Larson (2006), it is language teachers' responsibility to help their language learners build positive relationships with the target language and to create knowledge that would keep them engaged and highly motivated to continue in the language program, because students who are "cognitively engaged in language learning will be motivated to study for the long term and become lifelong users and learners of the foreign language" (p. 57). However, with the shift in emphasis from language teaching to language learning, Steinhart (2006) would like to see foreign language learners using the target language to explore and become knowledgeable about the part of the world where the host language is spoken, "with its linguistic, historical, contemporary, literary, and cultural variations" (p. 261).

In a study that discussed Iranian learners' attitudes and motivations toward learning EFL at the university level in Iran, Sayadian and Lashkarian (2010) identified numerous societal and psychological factors that may have motivated the learners to reach a high level of achievement. They concluded that "integrative motivation is the dominant motivational orientation" (Sayadian & Lashkarian, 2010, p. 137) for those learners, even though their learning of English was oriented for instrumental reasons.

Motivation is an essential affective factor that is strongly linked to successful foreign language learning and use. A language learner who is highly motivated to learn the language is "goal oriented, expends effort, is persistent, is attentive, has desires, exhibits positive affect, is aroused, has expectancies, demonstrates self-confidence, and has reasons" (Gardner, as cited in Comanaru, 2009, p. 133).

Literature Related to the Method

While past research studies were essential in exploring the methodology for the current study under investigation, they did not discuss the perceptions of Arab American high school students of Arabic about learning Arabic language and culture at any level. Also absent was describing the past experiences of teachers of Arabic as a foreign language at the secondary level. What the research revealed was an exploration on the perceptions and beliefs of college faculty and administrators about the role of foreign language (Wilkerson, 2006), as well as the perceptions, views, opinions, and attitudes toward language study in general (Payne, 2007). Furthermore, learners' perceptions about corrective feedback in Arabic foreign language classrooms were analyzed in order to see if the learners were able to demonstrate a thorough understanding of the intentions of the teachers who provided comments about specific linguistic episodes (Mackey et al., 2007).

In addition, past literature also revealed a casestudy of a European American graduate student who achieved a native-like and superior oral proficiency in Arabic (Samimy, 2008). Literature related to current qualitative methodology also explored the role of culture and literacy in maintaining heritage languages and rationale for foreign language acquisition at the university level (Sehlaoui, 2008), the need for language teachers to encourage their students to continue with foreign language study (Ketchum, 2006), as well as the role of foreign and multicultural language education in helping language educators understand the complexities of teaching culture (Fox & Diaz-Greenberg, 2006).

In a case study research examining teachers' perceptions and beliefs regarding their teaching methodologies, behaviors, actions, and practice for language teaching, Lorduy, Lambrano, Garces, and Bejarano (2009) studied five public secondary schools in Montaría, Colombia, through utilizing two instruments: interviews and recorded observations. The purpose of interviewing two of the five teachers was to collect information about their past experiences in their language classrooms, the tasks and activities employed to facilitate the learning, as well as the teaching methodologies they practiced. Also, the researchers observed the two teachers in their classrooms in order to compare and contrast their responses during the interviews and their teaching practice. The results of the study indicated that every teacher had his or her own way of delivering the lesson; the teachers strongly believed that the activities, materials, as well as other resources they used in class could have been mediated by their personal beliefs.

Literature also revealed a cross-case study investigating two teenage African American girls' past experiences with learning mathematics in school and the impact those experiences had on the motivation to study mathematics. Lim (2008) based the study on "repeated in-depth interviews and ethnographic observation of their mathematics classroom" (p. 303) in order to understand the social and cultural influences that affect minority learners' experiences in learning mathematics. The study was conducted in a middle school in the southeastern United States. The researcher used three types of data: participant observation, repeated interviews with the sixth-grade math teacher and eight other students, as well as school records. The findings of the study revealed that ethnicity, gender, and class influenced the two African American girls' experiences with learning mathematics; the young girls became demotivated to pursue a more advanced level of mathematical knowledge.

Moreover, a two-year longitudinal case study was conducted by Askham (2008) to explore adult learners' firsthand experiences regarding higher education in order to develop better learning infrastructure that would meet the students' interests and needs. Multiple diaries and series of interviews, logs, and focus groups were utilized to collect data. The researcher confirmed that emotional intensity was attached to the students' learning experiences, but there was also "the need to focus on the positive as well as the negative" (Askham, 2008, p. 95).

Based on the premise that teachers build their personal values, attitudes, beliefs, and assumptions about diversity based on their past experiences, Merriam (as cited in S. Lee, Butler, & Tippins, 2007) conducted a qualitative casestudy to seek "in-depth understandings and insights into educational practices and its meanings of situation and context" (p. 44). In the study, two in-depth interviews with one first-grade teacher were conducted, audiotaped, transcribed, and then analyzed by rereading, reducing, coding, and sorting into themes. To reach credibility, transferability, and confirmability, the researchers used member checks, peer examination, thick description, and "data-based evidence to support interpretations" (S. Lee et al., 2007, p. 44). The findings indicated that English-limited learners and their parents need to improve their English language skills in order to communicate with the learners' teachers more effectively. The results also emphasized the importance of creating a safe learning environment for those students by avoiding stereotypes and supporting diversity in school so all can benefit and learn.

Last but not least, an artistic inquiry using in-depth interviews with six Egyptian Muslim women was conducted in order to determine what those women experience and express through dance (Toncy, 2008). Also, a qualitative research using notes and close observations about the types, content, and effect of messages communicated over the Arabic Internet was conducted due to the establishment of Internet networks in Arab countries (Bakkar, 2008).

Thus, this qualitative study used the casestudy tradition in an attempt to describe and reveal the past experiences as perceived by Arab American high school teachers who have taught first-level Arabic language learners. The researcher also sought the perceptions of teachers of Arabic about the teaching of Arabic and culture. More details on the tradition of casestudy are provided in Chapter Three.

Literature Related to Differing Methods

Previous research has been channeled toward investigating the affective factors of anxiety and motivation that played a significant but positive role in influencing the learning of Arabic by individual students (DeSanto, 2009). Also, the relationship between the level of achievement in Arabic listening skills and motivation among various groups of language learners was identified by Rahimi (2009). Moreover, potential differences among various English-speaking children from middle-class American homes versus bilingual Arabic-/English-speaking children from middle-class Lebanese homes were investigated in order to identify how both groups would derive solutions when they are engaged in problem-solving activities (Chami-Sather & Kretschmer, 2005).

More specifically, in a study exploring inconsistencies between the instructional approach of communicative language teaching (CLT) and its implementation in foreign language classrooms in two schools in India, Christ and Makarani (2009) utilized a two-phase mixed-method study in which 31 teachers were surveyed and six selected teachers were purposefully interviewed. Those interviews were conducted in order to seek the teachers' perceptions on how they implement CLT in their classrooms. The findings showed a positive attitude about CLT practices, despite the challenges—classroom size and instructional resources—the teachers had to face in order to meet the needs of all foreign language learners.

Furthermore, in a phenomenological study investigating three immigrant children's (arriving in the United States before the age of 13 or U.S.-born) ethnolinguistic experiences with interpersonal and educational contact, along with contact through media, Zhang (2009) explored factors that could contribute to those children's Mandarin maintenance because Mandarin has been "framed as one of the strategic languages along with Arab and other Middle Eastern languages" (p. 196). The researcher conducted interviews with twelve parents in order to identify their attitudes and practices on maintaining Mandarin as a heritage language with their children in private and public settings. The findings suggested that immigrant families' attitudes, practices, and parental teaching techniques were "the strongest variables that constantly predict children's competencies in and attitudes towards Mandarin" (Zhang, 2009, p. 205).

In another phenomenological research study aimed at analyzing perceptions of special and general education teachers regarding their preparation for achieving successful inclusion applications, where the coteaching approach takes place, Gürür and Uzuner (2010) conducted semistructured interviews with the classroom teachers, compiled reflective daily data sources, and arranged planning meetings. The data for this study were phenomenologically analyzed utilizing inductive analysis. The findings did not clarify the teachers' roles and responsibilities in relation to specific approaches that could be applied in inclusion classes.

Literature related to the phenomenology method also revealed a study by Tercanlioglu (2008) of five English student-teachers' feelings, experiences, and perceptions of their English-teaching education in order to identify satisfaction levels and quality factors regarding departmental issues. Data from this phenomenological qualitative research were collected from open-ended focus groups' taped interviews. The results of the study showed that the English-teacher education department did not accommodate many of the students' needs. The findings also suggested the need to reconsider and reevaluate the English-teacher education program at the university level.

In another study investigating the motivation of students studying EFL at the International School in Tripoli, Libya, Ghenghesh (2010) used a mixed-method approach in which 144 students from 35 nationalities and five teachers completed questionnaire surveys. The surveys were also followed by semistructured interviews with 20 of the students and three of the teachers. The results of the surveys indicated that foreign language learners become demotivated with age; older learners scored significantly lower "on the motivation scale and the interview data gave support to this finding" (Ghenghesh, 2010, p. 128).

Past research also revealed a study on the conflicting perceptions between language learners and language teachers regarding factors that could impact language learning in foreign language classrooms. In the study, Hawkey (2006) employed a combination of quantitative and qualitative data collection methods. Data were collected in seven case-study schools—elementary, middle, and high school—located in north, central, and southern Italy. Attitude questionnaires, interviews, focus groups, and classroom observations were conducted throughout the 2001–2002 school year. The results showed huge differences between the students' and teachers' views on many activities that were completed in the classes and on the use of grammar and pair work.

Furthermore, literature also revealed a quantitative research study in which a survey was employed to compare motivations and orientations of two groups of learners of Arabic as a world language (Husseinali, 2006). Another quantitative study used a 19-question paper survey to report language study motivation, goals, and attitudes of first-year language learners at two American universities (Reynold, Howard, & Deak, 2009).The results noted significant differences between both groups at both universities and raised important questions in relation to developing curricula for heterogeneous groups of learners at those universities.

In addition, an experiment examining automaticity, which leads to near-native mastery in language acquisition, was conducted on a group of intermediate-level students of Spanish at the university level (Ridder, Vangehuchten, & Gomez, 2007). Also, Riazi (2007) utilized a quantitative study utilizing a questionnaire to analyze the perceptions of female Arabic-speaking students majoring in English at a university in Qatar. Another quantitative research study (A. V. Brown, 2009) used a questionnaire to compare groups of learners of commonly taught languages and less commonly taught languages at the university level in introductory-level courses.

Moreover, in a study investigating the levels of anxiety that heritage language students of Spanish experience while they learn Spanish in the classroom, Tallon (2009) employed a quantitative method approach using the Foreign Language Classroom Anxiety Scale. Data were collected from 209 heritage Spanish students and 204 nonheritage students. The findings showed that heritage language students experienced lower anxiety scores than nonheritage students, which in turn may explain why "some people are more successful at learning a second language than other people" (Tallon, 2009, p. 113).

Lastly, using quantitative methodology, Wen-Chi and Pin-Hsiang (2008) explored the views, opinions, and perceptions of Taiwanese university students regarding the learning environment—physical, social, and instructional—in their EFL classroom. Data collected from 593 freshman students who completed a survey concluded that the three aspects of the EFL learning environment were "considered by students to be an obstacle to their learning and that student motivation positively correlated with the learning environment" (Wen-Chi & Pin-Hsiang, 2008, p. 211).

Conclusion

As the world marks the turn of the twenty-first century, major changes have taken place in the teaching of foreign languages in U.S. schools, especially when the National Standards for the teaching of foreign languages were endorsed in schools across the nation. The rise in enrollment in foreign language programs and the growth of an ever-changing global society have called for enhanced cultural awareness and understanding in and beyond school boundaries.

The learning standards, known as the five Cs, that were created by various teams of professional educators are communication, cultures, connections, comparisons, and communities. The learning standards define learning outcomes and state clearly what students and teachers should know and be able to do in the classroom (National Standards, 2006). Two of the five standards—cultures and connections—were given considerable attention and learning credentials because learners' development of their language proficiency should extend beyond the celebrations and trivial and shallow cultural learning in an attempt to reach a level of thorough understanding of the practices, products, and perspectives (three Ps) of the host culture being studied (Fox &Diaz-Greenberg, 2006).

The harmony and intertwining of language and culture in foreign/world language classrooms are captured when language learners are given ample "opportunities for critical reflection on the ways in which culture affects language acquisition and particularly when teaching students from backgrounds different from their own" (Fox &Diaz-Greenberg, 2006, p. 412).Thus, examining Vygotsky's sociocultural theory supplements and solidifies the notion of seeing language as culture, and vice versa.

Sociocultural theory's major tenet was based on the belief that thorough understanding of an individual requires understanding the social and cultural relationships of the individual's surroundings. That is, an individual is socially and culturally situated as he or she interacts and communicates with other people on a daily basis. Language learners acquire and become proficient in a language through collaborating with their peers in group learning situations under their teachers' use of the ZPD (Vygotsky, 1978, 1986).Learners are social beings; therefore, it would be quite impossible to learn a language without using it with other speakers and without becoming a member of the host linguistic group or community. Therefore, success or failure in attaining the goal of learning a language would necessitate a positive attitude toward the target community group. Thus, the learner's attitude toward the target community group becomes critical in creating a high level of motivation or total resentment to learning the target language and culture.

Furthermore, sociocultural theory asks for what Vygotsky(1986) called mediated actions or tools that mediate the physical (external) objects, any physical object, and signs oriented to mediate the psychological (internal) objects, such as verbal and nonverbal language. Both orientations must come together to develop the individual's higher mental functions, which in turn helps him or her to learn a language. This is important because, according to Vygotsky (1986), individuals learn a language through the transition from the external to the internal, which helps understand the significance of reinforcing the cultural nodes in the individual.

Language is the most essential medium through which language learners learn and acquire a language. The utterances used by learners include sense and meaning (Vygotsky, 1978, 1986); it is the harmony and the fusion between the individual (sense) and the communal (meaning) aspects that help develop the human cognition to emerge and cultural practices to be understood. Thus, learning a language goes beyond drilling, defining vocabulary words, grammar, syntax, morphology, or phonology; it happens only in a sociocultural setting. Language is a communal practice, where human relations are developed and enhanced through human interaction, direct, indirect, or vicarious practices and experiences (Vygotsky, 1978).

Motivation is an essential affective factor that is strongly linked to success for language learning and use. A language learner who is highly motivated to learn the language is "goal oriented, expends effort, is persistent, is attentive, has desires, exhibits positive affect, is aroused, has expectancies, demonstrates self-confidence, and has reasons" (Gardner, as cited in Comanaru, 2009, p. 133). Hence, to become proficient in a foreign language is to demonstrate ability to use the language learned. Language acquisition cannot exist without use; language acquisition and language use are concepts that "are so tightly intertwined as to be rendered effectively inseparable" (Firth & Wagner, 2007, p. 806).

To learn a language, one has to have the desire to want to invest and communicate with speakers of that linguistic and cultural community, which in turn is what language is used for (Gardner, 1985). Resentment, however, toward that target language group would impede learning the target language. Thus, understanding how language is used in the social and cultural context remains central and more crucial in foreign language learning, which in turn explains why "grammar-based pedagogy was largely abandoned in favor of a communicative language teaching approach in the mid-1970s" (Dewaele, 2008, p. 248). Foreign language learning cannot be restricted to syntax, morphology, or phonology. On the contrary, language use is naturally expanded within the sociocultural context. Therefore, language is a communal practice and a communal activity through which language learners define themselves.

The next chapter discusses details of the methodology chosen for this study and describes the data that were collected and how the data were analyzed.

CHAPTER THREE
METHODOLOGY

Introduction

The purpose of this qualitative case study was to investigate Arab American high school teachers' perceptions regarding developing cultural awareness of first-level Arabic language learners. Specifically, this case study research was designed to understand in depth how teachers of Arabic teach or have taught the concept of culture in their first-level Arabic language classrooms, as well as the relationship between language and culture acquisition. Hence, this study fills the gap in past literature for which no research related to Arab American high school teachers of Arabic language and culture was conducted.

Chapter Three explains in detail the overall objective for assessing the quality of this qualitative research study. Also, the two senior high schools where the investigation took place are briefly described and the participants identified. In addition, this chapter discusses the data collection methods, data analysis and interpretation, and measures to ensure internal validity. Finally, it discusses privacy and other ethical issues and considerations.

Research Design

Merriam and Associates (2002) defined *qualitative study* as "an intensive holistic description and analysis of a single stance, phenomenology, or social unit" (p. 21). The case study qualitative paradigm was selected because it is a design that concentrates on understanding individuals' perceptions, past experiences, complex social phenomena (Yin, 2009), as well as different qualitative investigational perspectives and opinions about a specific situation or issue under examination (Creswell, 2007). According to Teachers of English to Speakers of Other Languages (n.d.), casestudy design has its origins in psychology and linguistics; however, more recently, it has been widely adopted in the field of education due to its emphasis on "issues related to learners' and teachers' identities, skill development and its consequences for learners, teachers' professional development experiences, and the implementation of language policies in programs and countries" (p. 1).

Moreover, Merriam and Associates (2002) and Stake (1995, 2000) explained that what constitutes a case study is the utmost concentration on the unit of analysis rather than the topic under investigation. In this study, we have chosen the casestudy design because it involves a thorough and intensive description, analysis, and interpretation of a social unit, "such as an individual, group, institution, or community" (Merriam & Associates, 2002, p. 8). According to Hatch (2002), whether a researcher chooses to undertake one single casestudy or a multiple casestudy research, he or she must collect specific details during data collection, "then set about the process of looking for patterns of relationship among the specifics" (p. 10).

Furthermore, Yin (2003) noted that when a researcher uses two or more case studies, the "chances of doing a good case will be better than using a single-case design" (p. 53). Thus, consistent with case study methodology, this current research involved the study of an issue/unit of analysis (Arabic culture in first-level Arabic language classes) through a total of five experiences/cases bounded by time (during the fall semester of the 2011 school year) and space (two high schools within the same district). Since the focus was on understanding how Arab American high school teachers of Arabic have experienced teaching Arabic culture in first-level Arabic classes, a casestudy inquiry was most suitable to adapt; it allowed us to "show different perspectives of the issue" (Creswell, 2007, p. 74). The purpose, then, of developing a research study based on interviews was "to learn more about the in-depth experiences of the participants" (Turner, 2010, p. 755).

For this study, inquiring about the inclusion of Arabic culture in first-level Arabic language classes at the high school level could improve foreign language teaching practice. Through one-on-one in-depth interviews, the issue/topic was experienced from the first-person perspective of Arab American high school teachers of Arabic as they reflected on the meaning of their current or previous experiences of teaching the language. Thus, interviewing teachers was essential, if not critical, because in examining the issue of developing cultural awareness in first-level Arabic classes from the teachers' own perspectives, the researcher may have been able to understand that learning a world language in itself is determined and dependent on the presence of a teacher. According to Peters (2009), Heidegger believed that teaching is complicated and far more difficult to do than learning "because what teaching calls for is this: to let learn" (p. 15).

Subjectivity is considered to be of utmost importance since it was the perceptions of those teachers that were counted on for understanding in depth how learning the Arabic language was projected in the past. Levering (2006) stated that "not only are people characterized as a unity of present, past, and future; they are also capable of retrieving the past" (p. 454). Thus, for this study, the teachers were able to reflect on their past experiences as they revealed how they think, learn, and question, for "the spoken word is greatly superior to the written" (Gray, as cited in Peters, 2009, p. 15).

As the researchers of this study, we were fully aware that this study could be approached using other qualitative designs, such as phenomenology, grounded theory, ethnography, and biography; however, there are many reasons for excluding these traditions. First, we considered the phenomenology design unsatisfactory due to the fact that "phenomenology attends to how people experience phenomena existentially" (Merriam & Associates, 2002, p. 97). According to Lukenchuk (2006), the term *phenomenology* was developed "in order to describe the science of appearances" (p. 426). Similarly, according to Shank (2006), phenomenology is a process whereby "we come to know things by the impact those things have upon our consciousness" (p. 131). In phenomenology, then, researchers seek to explore the essence of the lived experiences of the informants (Moustakas, 1994); however, in this study, there was no specific phenomenon to explore and we neither examined nor described or analyzed the teachers' everyday individual experiences. Likewise, we also dismissed the choice of ethnography because the current investigation neither called for observing a social or cultural group in a natural setting for a prolonged period of time nor for interpreting the teachers' detailed daily lives (Creswell, 1998, 2003). On the contrary, this study explored high school teachers' reflections regarding their teaching of Arabic culture to first-level Arabic language learners. Besides, the ethnographic tradition would also require that the information on the culture of a particular group be collected via observation and interview, which in turn was not what we were interested in exploring. In fact, we were more interested in describing, analyzing, and interpreting an issue through multiple viewpoints because that would permit broader interpretation of the participants—the teachers.

Also, the biographical tradition was dismissed for this study because the intention was not to explore the life of any individual who would choose to participate in the study but rather was concerned with the past "experiences for several individuals about a concept or a phenomenon" (Hatch, 2002, p. 51).

Finally, in a grounded theory, the researcher "attempts to derive a general, abstract theory of a process, action, or interaction grounded in the views of participants in a study" (Creswell, 2003, p. 14). If the primary outcome of this study were to develop a theory through interviewing a sampling of informants who represented diverse perspectives or if the aim were to have them observed in their schools, a grounded theory could have been chosen. However, the desire of the researcher was not to study "how people act and react to a phenomenon" (Creswell, 1998, p. 56), but to explore and describe the meaning of the experiences of the teachers only (Creswell, 2003, 2005; Merriam & Associates, 2002).

On the other hand, quantitative research was not the most appropriate approach in this research study since the researcher had identified a specific issue or unit of analysis (Creswell, 2003, 2005, 2007; Merriam, 1998) to understand and had chosen the individuals who may have been able to provide a detailed and lengthy description of what they had experienced (textual description of the experience), and how or in what context they had experienced that phenomenon (structural description of the experience; Creswell, 1998, 2003). While qualitative research is centered on textual data, quantitative research emphasizes numerical data, formulating hypotheses, designing surveys, and conducting experimental research, which in turn requires using control and treatment groups. Also, in quantitative research, the participants would have had to be randomly selected for a particular group and the findings carefully and systematically analyzed and interpreted (Duffy & Chenail, 2008). Thus, quantitative research was rejected because it would have provided neither detailed descriptions of the issue under examination by the participants in this study nor allowed "for depth of personal expression, emotionality, immediacy, and richness in detail in the collection of data" (Duffy & Chenail, 2008, p. 31).

Still, we did not perceive qualitative research as an easier method. In fact, qualitative data are not easy to collect, produce, analyze, or interpret because they "require judgment decisions" (Hsu, 2005, p. 131) that researchers with no previous research experience may not be able to handle properly. However, we tried to reach the goal, which was not to reflect on the participants' experiences in numbers but rather to search for understanding the personal meanings (Merriam & Associates, 2002) of the teachers' teaching experiences of Arabic culture in first-level Arabic language classes. In short, in this current study, we were "searching for understanding rather than knowledge; for interpretations rather than measurements; for values rather than facts" (Coleman & Briggs, 2006, p. 267).

Research Questions

Because this qualitative case study and data collection relied heavily on interviewing, we prepared a "fairly focused purpose, a fairly narrow set of research questions and a fairly well-structured data set in terms of its organization around a set of fairly consistent guided question" (Hatch, 2002, p. 152). The primary question with its sub-questions guiding the study was, "How do Arabic language teachers develop Arabic cultural awareness in first-level high school Arab language learners?"
1. What are Arabic language teachers' perceptions regarding the inclusion of cultural awareness in first-level Arabic language classes?
2. What cultural activities do Arabic language teachers implement in an effort to generate cultural awareness in first-level Arab language classes?

Context of the Study

Since this was a qualitative casestudy, emphasis was given to the amount and richness of detail obtained (through identifying important themes or patterns in the data) in order to explore the teachers' **perceptions regarding the single unit of analysis** (Merriam & Associates, 2002) under examination (developing cultural awareness of first-level Arabic language learners). Thus, data collection consisted of semi-structured in-depth interviews (formal and informal types of questions) with five high school teachers of Arabic as a foreign language.

In order to select participants for the interviews, we chose convenience sampling because of the participants' convenient accessibility (Wong & Chan, 2010). To ensure anonymity and protect the participants' identities, teachers were given pseudonyms.

Creswell (2003, 2005, 2009) and Iwamoto, Creswell, and Caldwell (2007) noted that face-to-face interviews are necessary when the researcher is not able to observe the participants closely. Similarly, Turner (2010) asserted that "interviews provide in-depth information pertaining to participants' experiences and viewpoints of a particular topic"(p. 754). For the purpose of this study, we conducted semi-structured in-depth interviews with high school teachers of Arabic because such interviews"contain a mix of more and less structured questions" (Merriam & Associates, 2002, p. 13). Through guided questions, the semi-structured interviews were also in-depth interviews because they were designed to deeply understand the informants' experiences regarding learning and teaching Arabic as a foreign language (Hatch, 2002). Thus, semi-structured in-depth interviews yielded the most relevant information because they kept the conversation alive, which in turn gave me the opportunity to explore the teachers' perceptions in greater depth through observing and recording their nonverbal expressions and language.

In planning this research study, we first sought approval from the school district's Office of Assessment and Evaluation and the two high school principals before approaching the teachers. We recruited the teachers through my personal e-mail account. Recruiting teachers took two weeks, so they were able to review the information and ask any questions before the actual interviews took place. The e-mail provided the teachers with information outlining the purpose of this research study, the nature of their participation, as well as my contact information for further details. To proceed with the study, the five high school teachers who currently teach Arabic as a foreign language at both high schools within the same district had to sign a consent form before the actual interviews took place.

The purpose behind interviewing the five high school teachers of Arabic was to understand how culture was integrated and represented in the first-level Arabic language classrooms, what instructional practices and teaching methodologies were being implemented, as well as what aspects of culture (practices, products, and perspectives) were being taught to students in their Arabic classes. Rubin (2005) stated that the researcher must look for "encultured informants, individuals who know the culture well and take it as their responsibility to explain what it means" (p. 66). The intent, therefore, was to allow for fuller and more thorough understanding of the case that was examined. The timeline for recruiting teachers was two weeks, plus two weeks for conducting the interviews. The semi-structured in-depth interviews with the teachers who taught Arabic at the first high school (SHSA) were conducted in classrooms located in the same school, whereas the interviews with the teachers who taught Arabic at the second high school (SHSB) were conducted at SHSB in each teacher's classroom. All interviews took place on school days after school hours. The teachers' interviews were 20–30 minutes in length.

The semi-structured in-depth interviews with the five teachers of Arabic consisted of a set of 20 open-ended questions. Follow-up and probe questions were determined by the teachers' responses to the questions. In order to examine the teachers' beliefs in detail and understand in depth the meanings of their teaching experiences of Arabic culture to first-level Arabic language learners, each teacher interview concentrated on the following four categories: exploration of the teachers' personal views on the term *culture* to understand how that belief had influenced and still influences the way they develop cultural awareness in first-level Arabic language classes (Q 1–8); description of the standard of culture and how this knowledge impacts the Arabic teaching field (Q 9–12); adapting and creating suitable language and cultural materials and methodologies appropriate to the cultural needs of the students (Q 13–16); and reflections and recommendations regarding the teaching and learning of cultural awareness in first-level Arabic language classes(Q 17–20).

In order to conduct professional interviews with the teachers, we needed to prepare for the interview. Hence, the quality of the data collected in the series of interviews, as Fox and Diaz-Greenberg (2006) explained, will:

> depend on both the interview design and on the skill of the interviewer. For example, a poorly designed interview may include leading questions or questions that are not understood by the participant. A poor interviewer may consciously or unconsciously influence the responses that the participant makes. In either circumstance, the research findings will be influenced detrimentally. (p. 5)

As the researchers, we were the only ones implementing the interviews (Creswell, 2003, 2007). To implement an interview is to actually make sure that the tape recorder is working properly, that we would ask the interviewee one question at a time, that we stay in control of the interview but neutral in order to eliminate any biases, and that we provide transition between the topics discussed. We also used an Interview Protocol for recording information during the interview. The Protocol included "a heading, instructions to the interviewer, the key research questions, probes to follow key questions, transition messages for the interviewer, space for recording the interviewer's comments" (Creswell, 2003, p. 190). Creswell (2007) and Turner (2010) also advised researchers to construct questions in order to avoid misunderstandings and to prepare follow-up questions or prompts so that optimal and detailed responses are obtained.

Additionally, conducting a successful interview demands accuracy on the part of the researcher and the participants. As mentioned earlier, all the interviews were tape recorded to maintain clarity and accuracy of the conversations as well as to allow us to give our undivided attention to the interview itself. Also, we complemented the data with field notes during the interviews in order to record the participants' facial expressions and gestures. These notes, as Creswell (2003, 2007) assured, helped us to keep track of the guiding questions that were addressed and see where we would go next with the interview. The teachers were assured that they could stop the recording to change, modify, or skip questions, or delete answers if they so desired.

The interviews consisted of specific questions prepared ahead of time as well as questions that were not predetermined because the study was designed to comprehend in depth how teaching Arabic culture to first-level Arabic language learners was experienced by each informant. Hatch (2002) noted that "although researchers come to the interview with guiding questions, they are open to following the leads of informants and probing into areas that arise during interview interactions" (p. 94).

While it was true that we, as researchers, considered sharing our own personal experiences as a starting point, we were also "concerned about saying something about reality 'as such'" (Levering, 2006, p. 456).

Measures for Ethical Protection of the Participants

Conducting qualitative research in an ethical manner made the current research a worthy one; the research depended largely on the researcher's own ethics and values, especially during the collection of data and the dissemination of the findings (Merriam & Associates, 2002). Respecting the participants' feelings is not only an ethical responsibility but also "an ethical imperative," as Hatch (2002, p. 66) put it. In this study, what the teachers said or expressed remained true because, as a qualitative researchers, we "can do no other but take what people say and think very seriously" (Levering, 2006, p. 457).

Before collecting data, we sought approval for this study from the school district's Office of Assessment and Evaluation, the two high school principals. We also ensured that the teachers' consent forms were signed and returned to us. Moreover, the names of the two schools involved in the study and those of the informants were never released but rather given pseudonyms to ensure privacy and maintain confidentiality so were able to build rapport with the respondents (Creswell, 2003, 2005, 2007).

Role of the Researcher

Professional Roles and Relationships

It was our sole responsibility to ensure that the names of all the informants remain anonymous and that the teachers' participation in the study was voluntary. Also, hard copies of the typed transcripts as well as the interview cassettes were kept locked in a file cabinet for protection until the entire study was completed. The study was saved on the researcher's password protected personal laptop, where no one could have access for a period of five years, at which time the data will be destroyed.

Methods for Establishing a Researcher-participant Relationship

The researcher had the obligation of informing the staff members that their participation in the study was entirely voluntary. Assuring the informants—teachers—that it was their absolute right to withdraw from the study at any in time, even after they signed the consent forms, was necessary in order to gain and maintain trustworthiness of the study. With that in mind, we made no further attempt to contact any teacher who did not wish to participate in the study. Hence, ethical issues regarding the collection of data and reporting of the findings were likely to emerge; however, "overlaying both the collection of data and the dissemination of findings is the researcher–participant relationship" (Merriam & Associates, 2002, p. 29).

Also, because this study required a certain level of active involvement and collaboration from staff members, and because they were asked to "reveal what goes on behind the scenes in their everyday lives" (Hatch, 2002, p. 66), a researcher–participant relationship of trustworthiness was established so the teachers could choose to be part of the study or opt out of it. Hence, the consent forms were mandated in order to protect the participants in the study from any emotional or physical harm (Creswell, 2003, 2005, 2007, Merriam & Associates, 2002). Moreover, in this study, after we transcribed the interviews, we gave each participant a written transcript of his or her interview to ensure accuracy. Based on the comments provided by those interviewed, we made the necessary modifications, changes, and conclusions.

Researcher's Experiences/Biases

The most essential and primary instrument in any study is the researcher (Creswell, 2003, 2007; Merriam & Associates, 2002; Patton, 2002). Qualitative research is subjective and interpretive in nature. This means that "the researcher filters the data through a personal lens" (Creswell, 2003, p. 182). As a researcher-interviewer (Merriam & Associates, 2002), it was difficult for us to set aside our own biases, which in turn affects the generalizability of this case study's findings. Hence, since we were the only people who prepared the consent forms; conducted and transcribed the interviews; gathered, analyzed, and interpreted the data; and reported the findings of the study, we tried to strengthen the study through avoiding "selective attention to details and selective interpretation of data" (Merriam & Associates, 2002, p. 147) and employing a variety of unique experiences contributed by the teachers who participated in this study. Finally, no controversial issues were discussed with any informant in order to avoid biases, and my own personal values were neither, directly or indirectly, disseminated.

Criteria for Selecting Participants

In a casestudy, it is imperative to focus on the meanings of the informants' experiences (Creswell, 2003, 2005, 2007, 2009). In this study, convenience sampling was used in order to ensure that all teachers selected to participate in the study met the same criteria:
1. High school teachers who teach or have taught Arabic as a foreign language to first-level Arabic language learners. First-level Arabic consists of two levels: Arabic 1 (first semester) and Arabic 2 (second semester).
2. High school teachers of Arabic had a minimum of five years of teaching Arabic as a foreign language.
3. High school teachers of Arabic would agree to join the study and sign a consent form.

Data Collection Procedures

Senior High School A (SHSA)

SHSA offers a unique experience in the area of teaching Arabic as a world language. The Arabic program was launched in 1982 right after the Israeli invasion of Lebanon, which resulted in the immigration of Lebanese families to the Midwestern state in the United States for this study. Located in the heart of the largest Arab community outside the Middle East, over 90 percent of SHSA's 2,400 student body is of Arab background. This high percentage of Arab Americans has played a significant role in considering Arabic as a heritage language not only in the school but also in the district. Currently, the school offers four years of Arabic (Zehr, 2006).

Senior High School B (SHSB)

Located just west of a large metropolitan city, SHSB is a four-year comprehensive high school of approximately 1,750 students representing a multicultural and diverse population including Native Americans, African Americans, Middle Easterners, Hispanics, and Asians (Zehr, 2006). This school was selected because it is the second high school within the same district that offers Arabic as a foreign language.

Before the study took place, we contacted the school district's human resources department in order to obtain approval from the school district's Office of Assessment and Evaluation to conduct the study at both high schools. As mentioned earlier, we used our personal e-mail accounts to contact the five teachers of Arabic at both high schools. The goal was to explain the study and seek their approval to participate in the study.

Thus, the convenience sampling helped us conduct one-on-one semi-structured in-depth interviews with a reasonable number of participants. The five teachers who voluntarily chose to participate in this study signed a consent form that addressed the following:
1. The nature and the purpose of the study. (On the day of each interview, we again reviewed the nature and the purpose of the study.)
2. The teacher's right to voluntarily accept or decline participating in the study at any time.
3. The date and the procedures of the study.
4. The amount of time needed to complete the interview.
5. Statements considering ethics, confidentiality, privacy of the participants, and any known risks associated with the study.
6. The social impact and anticipated benefits of participation.
7. Signatures of both the teacher and the researcher "agreeing to these provisions" (Creswell, 2003, p. 65).

Data Analysis

The purpose of this qualitative casestudy inquiry was to investigate Arab American high school teachers of Arabic regarding developing cultural awareness in first-level Arabic language classes. By adopting the case study tradition, we were able to answer the research questions and explore the meaning of the teachers' perceptions about teaching Arabic culture to first-level Arabic language learners. Thus, pursuing a casestudy investigation required that certain verb phrases such as *to be heard* and *to be seen* became part of the analysis (Friesen, Feenberg, & Smith, 2009).

Additionally, because this research was a casestudy, it utilized semi-structured one-on-one in-depth interviews that resulted in a huge amount of data, which began "from the first moments of data collection" (Hatch, 2002, p. 149). The researchers also noted that analyzing and interpreting the collected data through interviews started after they transcribed verbatim the recorded interviews within 48 hours of collecting the data.

Data analysis in qualitative research is simultaneous with data collection (Merriam & Associates, 2002). In this study, data analysis started with the first interview; it allowed us to change, modify, and adjust along the way. Creswell (2003, 2005) also advised qualitative researchers not to wait until all data are collected because they might lose the possibility of gathering other important details in the data.

According to Seidel (1998), qualitative data analysis is a process of *"noticing, collecting, and thinking* about interesting things" (p. 1). The relationship among these three parts is "an infinite spiral" (Seidel, 1998, p. 2) because they are interlinked. Figure 3.1 represents the basic process of qualitative data analysis and the relationship among the three parts.

To elaborate, Seidel (1998) argued that when a researcher does qualitative data analysis, he or she does not notice, collect, then think about interesting things, then write a report; the process is, rather, iterative and progressive because it is a cycle; recursive because as the researcher is busy collecting things, he or she might notice or discover new things to collect; and holographic because every step taken in the process will always have these three parts combined. In this study, therefore, as we noticed things, we were also collecting and thinking about interesting things along the way.

Figure 3.1. Qualitative Data Analysis (Seidel, 1998)

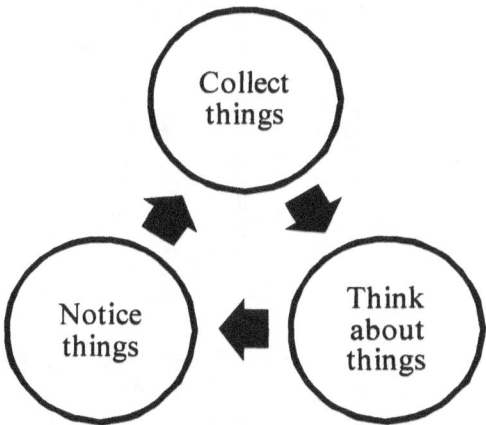

More specifically, during interviews, we watched, listened to what the interviewee was saying, tape recorded, as well as made observations of his or her nonverbal language and expressions. Hence, we recorded things that we noticed during the interviews. Then, we read what we recorded many times to discover new and interesting things in the record. When we had identified those interesting things, we assigned them a code (Seidel, 1998). The second step involved collecting and sifting through the data, and sorting through the recorded notes to classify the codes in groups. The last step was to think about the things or to examine the things we had collected in order to understand, search for patterns, as well as to make preliminary discoveries about the topic/issue under investigation. In other words, after sorting/classifying data was completed, we reviewed each piece individually in order to compare and contrast the things we noticed, identified any similarities or differences among them, and found sequence and patterns in order to reassemble the data in a meaningful way (Seidel, 1998). Thus, this qualitative case study utilized the following data analysis process, which we designed based on Seidel (1998).

Figure 3.2. Process of Data Analysis in this Qualitative Case Study (Seidel, 1998)

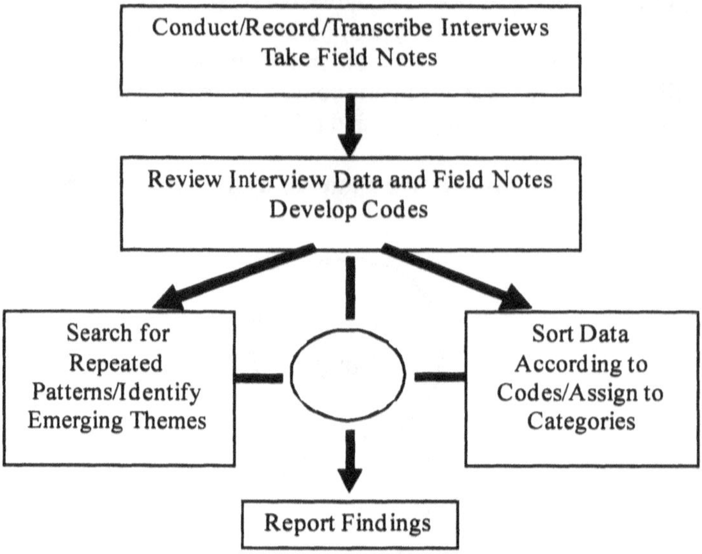

```
┌─────────────────────────────────────┐
│ Conduct/Record/Transcribe Interviews │
│         Take Field Notes             │
└─────────────────────────────────────┘
                  │
                  ▼
┌─────────────────────────────────────┐
│  Review Interview Data and Field Notes │
│            Develop Codes             │
└─────────────────────────────────────┘
          │        │        │
          ▼        ▼        ▼
┌──────────────┐      ┌──────────────┐
│  Search for  │      │  Sort Data   │
│   Repeated   │──○──│ According to │
│ Patterns/Identify │      │Codes/Assign to│
│ Emerging Themes │      │  Categories  │
└──────────────┘      └──────────────┘
                  │
                  ▼
          ┌───────────────┐
          │ Report Findings │
          └───────────────┘
```

Coding data. Data analysis first started with our tape recording and transcribing all the interview data. It also involved reviewing the field notes that were taken during the interviews. Topic codes were also developed based on the emerging categories (Seidel, 1998).

Sorting data. Based on the topic codes that were assigned to the categories, data were broken up into smaller pieces and in turn relocated and placed into the categories (Seidel, 1998).

Analyzing data. When data were sorted and categorized, searching for any repeated patterns among the topic codes in every category and across all the categories in order to locate and identify the emerging themes (Seidel, 1998) began. Creswell (2007) noted that themes are aggregated together for the purpose of developing major ideas in the collected data. This stage also included looking for the quotes in the transcribed interviews that supported the recurring themes from the interview data. The recurring themes are listed and discussed later in Chapter Four.

Reporting the findings. The results of this qualitative casestudy are reported and discussed thoroughly in Chapter Four.

Methods to Address Validity

Because the study employed the meaning of the experiences of high school Arab American teachers of Arabic language and culture through interviewing, it had "a high degree of what is technically labeled *validity*" (Smeyers, 2008, p. 696). The findings of this casestudy had three essential ingredients: credibility, confirmability, and transferability. Tercanlioglu (2008) defined *credibility* as "the confidence one can have in the truth of the findings and [credibility] can be established by various methods" (p. 143), such as member checking. He further defined *confirmability* as "the degree to which the results could be confirmed or corroborated by others" (Tercanlioglu, 2008, p. 143), through having someone review the transcribed interviews, themes generated, as well as data elimination or reduction to assure credibility. Lastly, he defined *transferability* as "the degree to which the results of qualitative research can be generalized and transferred to other contexts or settings" (Tercanlioglu, 2008, p. 144).

Merriam and Associates (2002) explained that in qualitative research, internal validity or reliability adds richness and strength to the research study and to the holistic analysis and interpretation of the informants' experiences. In this study, we utilized two of the most common strategies to reach internal validity: member checks—taking the preliminary interpretations and findings back to the informants from whom we "derived the raw data through interviews" (Merriam & Associates, 2002, p. 26) for better perspectives—and peer review—asking a doctoral candidate who was already very familiar with our research to "scan some of the raw data and assess whether the findings are plausible based on the data" (p. 26).

Additionally, one of the most challenging issues concerning casestudy research is for a qualitative researcher to be able to justify the study in terms of external validity or generalizability; however, Merriam and Associates (2002) pointed out that since small, non-random samples are selected purposefully in qualitative research, it is not possible to generalize statistically. A small sample is selected precisely because the researcher wishes to understand the particular in depth, not to find out what is generally true of the many. (p. 28)

Since this was a qualitative casestudy, generalizability was conceptualized through the readers who are the only ones who could determine if the findings could be applied or transferable to their context or situation (Merriam & Associates, 2002). Nevertheless, providing readers with rich, thick description (Creswell, 2003, 2005, 2007; Merriam & Associates, 2002; Turner, 2010) was our responsibility as the researchers of this study to ensure generalizability.

Another strategy to reach external validity is the use of multisite designs or maximizing variation in the purposely selected sample (Merriam & Associates, 2002). This study involved two sites (high schools) where Arabic language was taught as a foreign language. The teachers who chose to be interviewed were diverse because of the nature of the sites and the informants' various ethnic and cultural backgrounds.

Finally, maximizing validity of the findings of the study require the researcher to corroborate evidence and cross-check data (Coleman & Briggs, 2006) through many sources. As the researchers asserted, this study would achieve "triangulation within the interview method by interviewing" (Coleman & Briggs, 2006, p. 69) Arab American high school teachers of Arabic as a world language. This casestudy also established validity through including the audiotapes along with the researcher's field notes.

Conclusion

The purpose of this casestudy research was to investigate Arab American high school teachers' perceptions regarding developing cultural awareness in first-level Arabic language classes. A qualitative casestudy tradition was carried out since the teachers' beliefs and perceptions about the issue under examination were not "measurable [but rather] uncovered, described, and also explained" (Lorduy et al., 2009, pp. 36–37). The tools implemented in this study included semistructured in-depth interviews with five high school teachers of Arabic in the two high schools involved in this study.

Qualitative researchers need not "accept the misconception that more methods [mean] better or richer analysis" (Janesick, 2004, p. 106). It is the quality of the selected methods rather than the quantity that counts. It is also worth noting that subjectivity in the qualitative approach is embraced and serendipitous when "a tremendous amount of meaningful data" (Janesick, 2004, p. 108) fall into place to give a more powerful setting, content, and participants. The researcher's own reflexivity and self-reflection on various issues and the diversity among participants selected for the study were also of equal importance. Keeping field notes in tandem with audiotaping the interviews was done in the event that the tape recorder did not operate properly.

This chapter offered a detailed explanation of the tradition, design, paradigm, methodology, and steps and procedures required to initiate the research. Chapter Four explains thoroughly how the data of this study were collected, analyzed, and interpreted. Chapter Five provides an overview of the findings of the study, offers recommendations necessary to improve the existing Arabic program in the schools within the district, and provides a few points needed for further research concerning the challenges facing teachers who teach advanced levels of Arabic.

CHAPTER FOUR
RESULTS

Introduction

The purpose of this qualitative case study was to investigate Arab American high school teachers' perceptions regarding developing cultural awareness of first-level Arabic language learners. This chapter presents and analyzes the findings of the study in two parts. The first part reviews the research questions and offers a detailed explanation of the research process and the second part presents the findings of the teachers' transcribed interviews.

Research Process

During the Fall 2011, data were collected through one-on-one semi-structured interviews of five high school teachers who teach or have taught first-level Arabic language classes within the same district. The purpose of interviewing the teachers was to understand how culture is integrated in their first-level Arabic language classrooms, what instructional practices and teaching methodologies are implemented, as well as what aspects of culture—**practices, products, and perspectives**—are taught to develop cultural awareness in first-level Arabic language classes.

After obtaining approval from the district's Office of Assessment and Evaluation and the two high school principals, we sent an e-mail to all five high school teachers of Arabic at the two research sites with information outlining the purpose of this research study, the nature of their participation, as well as my contact information for further details. An initial meeting was held after school the following week in both high schools to further explain and discuss this qualitative case study. All five teachers signed the consent form before the actual interview took place. The consent form included a description of the nature and purpose of the research study; the teacher's individual right to voluntarily accept or withdraw from the study at any time; the date and procedures of the study; the amount of time allocated to conduct the interview; and statements regarding ethics, privacy of the participants, the social impact and anticipated future benefits of the research study. The form required the signatures of both the participant and the researcher.

Data collection involved the teachers' semi-structured audio-taped interviews, which were conducted after school hours at the two research sites during the second and third weeks of October 2011. The interviews were expected to be 20 to 30 minutes long, but the actual interviews ranged from 10 to 20 minutes in length. The interviews with the SHSA teachers were held in the researcher's classroom at SHSA and the SHSB teachers' interviews were conducted in their classrooms at SHSB. During the interviews, each teacher was asked a series of 20 open-ended questions. The questions were designed to align with the primary question and its two sub-questions. Each audio-taped interview was repeatedly reviewed before it was transcribed. The transcribed interviews were also reviewed by the teachers a week later to ensure accuracy. Data were gathered and analyzed to answer the following primary research question and its two sub-questions:
- How do Arabic language teachers develop Arabic cultural awareness in first-level high school Arab language learners?
    1. What are Arabic language teachers' perceptions regarding the inclusion of cultural awareness in first-level Arabic language classes?
    2. What cultural activities do Arabic language teachers implement in an effort to generate cultural awareness in first-level Arab language classes?

Data Analysis

The data collected, recorded, and analyzed were guided by the primary research question and its two sub-questions. Data analysis of this qualitative case study was based on Seidel's (1998) qualitative data analysis, which contains three interlinked parts: "*noticing, collecting, and thinking* about interesting things" (p. 1). During the interviews, we watched and listened to what the teachers were saying, tape recorded each interview using two tape recorders to avoid loss of data, and made specific observations—field notes—of the teachers' facial expressions and nonverbal language. After we recorded what we had noticed during the interviews, we read many times what we had recorded to discover new and interesting things in the record. When we finished identifying those items of interest, we gave them specific codes based on the data derived from the interview transcripts. The next step included recording the participants' facial expressions and gestures, collecting and sifting through the data, and sorting through the recorded notes to organize and classify the codes in groups. To be more specific, *open coding* followed by *axial coding* were used in the initial stage of analysis. Rubin and Rubin (2005) stated that coding allows researchers to "quickly locate excerpts from all the interviews that refer to the same concept, theme, and event" (p. 219). Hence, open coding started with assigning a code to meaningful segments and statements identified in the interview transcripts. When all text segments were highlighted and initial coding was completed and recorded on the left-hand side of each transcribed interview, we examined the codes and grouped them into themes. We also kept a master list of the 24 codes that were developed. Repetitive readings of the teachers' interviews resulted in the emergence of three significant themes and six subthemes among the data (see Table 4.1).

Table 4.1
Themes and Subthemes

Major Theme	Subthemes
Connecting language and culture	• Learning language in cultural context • Using various cultural resources
Developing culture learning	• Utilizing appropriate cultural learning strategies and activities • Assessing students' cultural learning
Improving culture learning and teaching	• Communicating with others • Addressing cultural learning challenges

In presenting the results of this research study, the five teachers' responses were aligned with each interview (Appendix D) to show support to the existing categories and help identify specific answers to the primary research question and two subquestions. Thus, qualitative data analysis provided a rich description of previous and/or current experiences of the five high school teachers of Arabic.

The Findings

Background Information

Each of the five Arab American teachers of Arabic who participated in this research study has been teaching Arabic in the same school district for at least 10 years. Three of the five teachers are Lebanese, one is Iraqi, and another is Palestinian. The teachers come from diverse cultural and ethnic backgrounds. All teachers have participated, at least twice each semester, in a series of district-wide professional development training sessions at the elementary, middle, and high school level to expand and improve the existing Arabic language program. The teachers also have been involved in developing and sharing common thematic lesson plans, unit tests, end-of-semester tests, and best practices to ensure that students are fully engaged and that learning is taking place according to the national foreign language standards, or the five Cs: communication, cultures, comparisons, connections, and communities.

The three major themes and the six subthemes that emerged from current or previous experiences shared by the Arab American high school teachers of Arabic who participated in this study are summarized in Table 4.2.

Table 4.2
Themes

Research Question	Themes
Primary: How do Arabic language teachers develop Arabic cultural awareness in first-level high school Arab language learners?	
1. Subquestion: What are Arabic language teachers' perceptions regarding the inclusion of cultural awareness in first-level Arabic language classes?	• Connecting language and culture • Improving culture learning and teaching
2. Subquestion: What cultural activities do Arabic language teachers implement in an effort to generate cultural awareness in first-level Arab language classes?	• Developing culture learning

Theme 1: Connecting Language and Culture

Theme 1 relates to the Arab American high school teachers' understanding of the relationship between Arabic language and culture and how that connection may have informed them of better ways to teach language in a cultural context using various but more effective cultural resources. The findings of this theme are in response to the following interview questions:
1. How do you define *culture*/what does *culture* mean to you?
2. Do you believe learning Arabic language is different than learning Arabic culture?
3. Do you see a connection between the two?
4. What role does Arabic culture play in language learning?
5. Do you think first-level Arabic language learners should stay in touch with the culture of the language they are learning?
6. What is your overall teaching approach to Arabic culture?
7. How frequent is/was culture taught in your previous beginning Arabic class?
8. What learning resources did you rely on to teach Arabic culture?
9. How often did you use those cultural resources?

These interview questions were intended to answer the primary research question and first sub-question: How do Arabic language teachers develop Arabic cultural awareness in first-level high school Arab language learners? What are Arabic language teachers' perceptions regarding the inclusion of cultural awareness in first-level Arabic language classes? The teachers' responses to the aforementioned questions fell into two categories: learning language in cultural context and using various cultural resources, as outlined in Table 4.3.

Table 4.3
Theme 1: Connecting Language and Culture

Category	Responses
Learning language in cultural context	• Practice of cultural activities (TA, TB, TC, TD, TE) • Learning culture through social interaction (TA, TB, TC, TD, TE)
Using various cultural resources	• Using their own personal experience (TB, TD) • Taking students on cultural field trips (TA, TB, TC, TD, TE) • Using the internet for enhancing cultural knowledge (TA, TB, TC, TD, TE) • Exposing learners to various readings (TA, TB, TC, TD, TE)

Learning Language in Cultural Context

Jenkins (2009) stated that the term *culture* is viewed "as the symbolic vehicles of meaning and experience such as beliefs, ritual practices, artistic expression, traditions, and ceremonies" (p. 134). For the purpose of this research study, all five teachers shared a common perspective of *culture*. TA stated, "Culture is a way of life of given people. It would include language, dress, religion, traditions." TB defined culture as a way of life; it includes language, social activities, and practice by a group of people. Similarly, TC stated, "Culture can be defined by many aspects of our life, whether it is language, food, location, place."

> Culture is a combination of many components. It includes traditions, way of life, folklore tales, fables, foods, social interaction, the role of man and woman in the society, the way they raise their children, the common things that people share on a daily basis. (TD)

TE defined culture as "the practice of people, community, and traditions."

The participants indicated that there was a connection between the Arabic language and culture. TA stated that language and culture "can be intertwined in many ways" and believed that "learning the culture sometimes can help the student understand the language better and so in that case makes things a lot easier and clearer to the students." TB stated, "Language affects the culture and the culture affects language" and believed that "a good teacher is one who tries to introduce both at the same time." Similarly, TC said, "Arabic language is part of the Arabic culture. It is a continuation and they complete each other." This connection between language and culture can be found, TC added, "in every aspect of our daily life activities and, therefore, help the students connect with the language." TD commented that language and culture "have to be together." TE also stated that there is a very "strong connection" between the two because "it makes the language less intimidating and it makes it friendlier and also more comprehensive."

Teaching the Arabic language and developing cultural awareness in first-level Arabic language classes must always happen in cultural context, which was confirmed by all five teachers. TA said, "At least once a week, I give students a mini-lesson on culture and that can include making holiday cards, watching videos related to culture, show-and-tell, bringing things from home related to culture, sharing with students." TB stated that he introduces it in body language in a role-play activity such as the "TPR" (total physical response). He said, "I ask a student to come out and to try to act the situation. Two students are supposedly greeting. When two Arabs meet, how do they introduce each other, how do they greet each other?" TC said, "If we take food, many people are now familiar with the Middle Eastern cooking and, therefore, as one aspect of the culture, food can be a very helpful and it enlivens the language to the students." In other words, *food* serves as a vehicle to engage students in using the Arabic language. Similarly, TD introduces culture "through practices either in the class or in the community, like going on field trips." In class, TD introduces culture learning "through projects, reading folkloric tales, and watching movies." TE assured that culture is learned "in every lesson" and stated:

> We use segments of culture whenever appropriate. . . . Culture is introduced into the language lessons as smoothly as possible in a way that I don't make it look separable. I use the lesson, the theme, the language lesson as an occasion to present cultural aspects.

Using Various Cultural Resources

The participants utilize a variety of shared and different cultural resources to teach culture to first-level Arabic language learners. TA stated, "Besides bringing the show-and-tell items, the United Streaming has many good videos related to culture." When asked about what United Streaming is, TA explained that it is the Discovery Channel with a lot of educational videos. He stated, "You can just type to search a word or put in your subject matter, and it will give you a listing of those videos." TA stated that he/she relies on these resources "75 percent of the time." TB stated, "I rely heavily on my experience in addition to various books provided by the world language department." TC indicated that he relies on the Internet, books, field trips, and movies to teach beginners Arabic culture. Similarly, TD uses his/her personal experience as well as a cultural learning resource in addition to reading multiple folktales and going on trips to the Detroit Institute of Art and Arab American Museum. Finally, TE stated, "I rely so much on U-Tube and the Internet . . . 50 percent of the time, like, if I am teaching them five days, I use them two days."

Theme 2: Developing Culture Learning

Theme 2 relates to the teachers' implementation of various strategies, activities, and culture-teaching method to develop cultural awareness in first-level Arabic language classes. It also refers to the teachers' emphasis on assessing the students' learning of cultural elements that are essential to acquiring the Arabic language. All teachers used many but different tools for measuring the students' cultural learning, which in turn may have given both teachers and students a holistic look at their cultural progress and/or proficiency.

The findings of this theme were in response to the following interview questions:
1. How familiar are you with the practices, products, and perspectives (the three Ps) of culture?
2. Which of the three Ps were you most comfortable to teach and why?
3. In your opinion, what Arabic cultural knowledge did your Arab American students gain in their first year of Arabic? How do you know they did/did not?
4. What instructional practices/learning strategies did/do you utilize to facilitate developing cultural awareness in first-level Arabic classes?
5. How do/did you assess the students' cultural understanding of Arabic?

These questions were intended to answer the primary research question and first sub-question: How do Arabic language teachers develop Arabic cultural awareness in first-level high school Arab language learners? What cultural activities do Arabic language teachers implement in an effort to generate cultural awareness in first-level Arab language classes? The teachers' responses to the questions fell into two categories: utilizing appropriate cultural learning strategies and activities and assessing student cultural learning, as outlined in Table 4.4.

Table 4.4
Theme 2: Developing Culture Learning

Category	Responses
Utilizing appropriate cultural learning strategies and activities	• Utilizing differentiating instruction (TC) • Body language (Total Physical Response/TPR) (TB) • Assigning individual and group work • Using lectures on cultural aspects (TB)
Assessing student cultural learning	• Fill-in-the-blank (TA, TB, TC, TD) • Oral practice (TA, TB, TC, TD, TE) • True/false (TA, TB, TC, TD) • Multiple-choice (TA, TB, TC, TD)

Chapter Four

Utilizing Appropriate Cultural Learning Strategies and Activities

All participants interviewed indicated that they felt more comfortable teaching the practices of culture than the products or perspectives, except for TB who stressed teaching the perspectives of the Arabic culture.

> I have been around various cultures of the Arab world and I know some of you know their practices, like, for example, the way maybe people in northern Iraq may wear a head gear differently than some people in southern Iraq.(TA)

TB stated:

> I try to put the students in a situation where they practice the culture through language. Like I mentioned before, I try, for instance, to show them how when two Arabs meet somewhere in the street or on a bus or at a restaurant, what kind of dialogue goes on, how they introduce each other. So this is how I try to seek the opportunity.

TB also paid attention to the learning of the perspectives of culture:

> *Perspectives* means values and, you know, those kids, I have to admit, there is a gap between the Arab values and the American values. As a teacher, I have to try to simplify so that the student would be aware about their own culture.

TC said, "One cannot learn any language without practice because it lays down the foundation of what I am going to be teaching." He concluded, "Practice is what makes it connect to all aspects with other perspectives." TD offered a similar line of thinking: "I like the *practices* one. It is like you really apply. You do it. You are not just lecturing about it. I feel more comfortable with the *practices* one." TD also provided the following example:

> When they come in the room, they have to greet me. It is not like they come and sit. They have to greet. The way they sit at their table, it has to be in a certain way because in the Arab culture, they are not supposed to, for example, stretch on the chair, put their feet on the table.

TE believed that the three Ps (practices, products, perspectives) are intertwined but that the teaching of the practices of culture is what she is most comfortable with because "it makes more sense to the students. It makes sense of the language. It makes language more real to them. It is authentic."

In addition, all teachers revealed that they incorporate a wide variety of learning strategies that focus on promoting cultural awareness in first-level Arabic language classes. TA mentioned that specific cultural strategies, such as show-and-tell, helped his/her first-level Arabic learners identify with their Arabic culture "because they were able to touch things and smell things." TA also mentioned that he/she sometimes wore cultural clothes to class to add authenticity to the teaching of culture. In addition, to enrich the students' cultural knowledge, he/she often discussed with students specific topics related to Arabic culture when introducing new vocabulary words. TA stated:

> With the end of Ramadan, we talked about holiday-related words. We talked about New Moon and some of the practices that go along with the celebrating the holiday. We made holiday cards. But if the students happened to be Christian, TA allowed the student to "make it out to the holiday that they celebrated.

Similarly, TB stated that teaching Arabic as a foreign language is tough and that is why he has "always come wearing different hats to the classroom." TB assured that he tries to simplify teaching Arabic by being "funny sometimes in order to introduce it to the students." Like TA, TB relies on "lecturing sometimes" to introduce a specific cultural aspect of the language. He enjoys teaching culture in context and stated:

> I put them in situations. What I am trying, for instance, this year, I try a very short play and put them in situations, for instance, how to act in different situations when you go, for instance, into a house, when you are invited for dinner, or for a wedding.

TC preferred to utilize the strategy of differentiating instruction:

> Differentiating instruction helps a lot, especially using the ability of advanced students to work with the students who are trying to learn the language and, therefore, this thing would help me in both ways: to stay in touch and to develop the ability.

Like TB, TD mentioned using specific vocabulary words and/or terms to practice culture and enhance the students' cultural awareness:

> In the first year of Arabic, I teach them, for example, how the Arabic people use the name of God frequently and it is not a taboo. If you do something, you say, "*Alhamdulillah*," meaning *thank God*. If somebody asks you about your well-being, you don't just say, "I am fine" but you say also, "Thank God. Am I going to see you tomorrow?" You don't just say yes or no, you say, "Yes, *inshallah*," meaning *if God wills*.

Some of the other instructional strategies TD also uses are "bell-work, group work, asking questions, discussions." Similarly, TE gave an example of how she introduces vocabulary words when covering a lesson on family. She makes the lesson culturally oriented. She said, "Like Arabic names. What is behind the name, the Arab family, the cousins to the mother's side and the father's side?" TE also said:

Ask them to prepare mini cultural lessons themselves . . . and every day I have 2 minutes at the beginning of the class where one student presents anything that is part of anything that is related to culture. They have that as part of their lesson.

Assessing Student Cultural Learning

In terms of assessing the students' **cultural knowledge**, all five teachers thought it essential to assess first-level Arabic language learners' cultural knowledge and skills appropriately and that those skills must reflect the cultural goals of Arabic as a foreign language. TA said, "**Sometimes on Fridays, I give them a notebook quiz** based on the lesson that we went over the notes that they took. I ask them 10 random questions." TB also gives "**fill-in-the-blanks**" tests. He said that he would give them a map of the Middle East with a list of the Arabic countries in English and then ask students to locate and write the name on the map. TC said, "I give them a weekly test on what we are working on, and sometimes it would be an oral test." When asked about the type of test he would give, TC emphasized both short-answer and multiple-choice tests in English.

> First, through regular evaluation with multiple-choice quiz, a true-or-false quiz, but also through practice. Like sometimes, I tell them to "Be very careful to the way you answer me, the way you greet me, the way you talk to me. I want to see that you are really practicing your culture in the classroom. (TD)

TE emphasized that she does not "**give them any written.** It is not summative but formative. It is from their discussion, watching how they discuss it, how they relate to it."

Theme 3: Improving Culture Learning and Teaching

Theme 3 relates to the teachers' perceptions regarding communicating with parents, the Arab community, and people from other cultures. It also refers to identifying certain challenges when teaching culture to first-level Arabic learners and taking immediate steps to improve practice with regard to culture teaching and learning in beginning Arabic classes. The findings of this theme were in response to the following interview questions:
1. Do you think it is important for teachers/students of Arabic to communicate with people from other cultures?
2. Have you encountered any persistent struggles/challenges with teaching the cultural component of the language?
3. Do you believe that culture learning can be achieved in the classroom?
4. What immediate steps should teachers of Arabic take to improve practice with regard to culture teaching and learning in first-level Arabic language classes?
5. In you opinion, do you think teachers of Arabic should familiarize themselves improve cultural awareness instruction?

6. Do you support the claim that culture in first-level Arabic language classes is still treated as a luxury rather than an integral component of the language?

These interview questions were intended to answer the primary research question and second sub-question: How do Arabic language teachers develop Arabic cultural awareness in first-level high school Arab language learners? What are Arabic language teachers' perceptions regarding the inclusion of cultural awareness in first-level Arabic language classes? The teachers' responses to these questions fell into two categories: communicating with others and addressing cultural learning challenges, as outlined in Table 4.5.

Table 4.5
Theme 3: Improving Culture Learning and Teaching

Category	Responses
Communicating with others	• Cooperate between school and home (TA, TB, TC, TD)
	• Invite community members to speak (TA, TB, TC, TD)
Addressing cultural learning challenges	• Understanding student sub-cultures (TA, TB, TC, TD, TD)
	• Lack of cultural materials (TA, TB, TC, TD, TE)
	• Students struggle between 2 cultures: American and Arabic (TA, TB, TC)

Communicating with Others

All five teachers indicated that it is absolutely important for them as educators and for students to communicate and interact with people from other cultures for the sake of appreciating, valuing, and accepting each other's **cultural differences and identities** (Bloom, 2008).

> It is very important because you learn some of the religions of other cultures. I currently have one Mexican student, I have two African American students and one Cuban student, and there is a lot of giving and taking in class. (TA)

TB emphasized the interaction among the students since they come from various Arab countries and backgrounds and from different cultures to learn more about their own and other people's history, traditions, and lifestyles. TB stated, "We sometimes come across this difficulty especially when we have students come from unstable situations, a political situation like in Iraq." TC said, "It is important to communicate with people of other cultures. They can understand their own culture and they will be opened up to the Arabic culture." TD also emphasized the importance of interacting among people of the same or various cultures in order to

Compare and contrast and see what positive sides of the culture exist.... We have to interact with some cultures that are somehow influenced by the Arabic culture to see how our culture influenced other cultures. Take the Spanish culture, for example; I like this interaction between cultures, and if you live in a country where you want to keep your culture and interact and live with another culture, you need to mix the two together.

TE stated:

It makes them understand themselves better and to understand other people and make it more successful, not only the relationships but also understanding some aspects of life in general, like, even in politics. We take it to a wider aspect of the world.

Although TA, TB, TC, and TD thought that teachers of Arabic should make every effort to understand their students' Arabic backgrounds by communicating with their parents and/or the rest of the community to which they belong, TE believed there is absolutely no need to go this far. TE stated, "I don't think so personally. I don't think they need to go there, to that extent, to inquire about the families related to students." TA, TB, and TD mentioned that inviting parents and other community members to their classes can play a positive role in advancing the students' cultural skills. TA said,"I think I would like to see the day where we can actually invite someone who may be an expert in a specific area to speak to first-level students—someone from the community." TB stated:

Parents also can help by enforcing what the teachers teach, and visitation between the parents and the teachers can help a lot, and the community can help also. For instance, like, what we did, if you remember once, we took the students to the Arab museum. We visited. They learned about the Arab culture when they came to this country, and the same time, we went together, teachers and the students, to [an Arab] bakery. They became familiar with the food Arabs are eating.

TC noted that he would like to practice this communication between school and home and teachers and parents on a "daily practice," while TD highly recommended getting "in touch with the community." TD added:

If you are a teacher of Arabic but not of Arabic heritage, it is a big necessity that you know about the culture, that you know about the society, you interact with the people in their houses. It is communication.

TD also thought that if first-level Arabic language learners happen to be of non-Arabic origin, it is the teacher's responsibility to "teach them this awareness of the Arabic culture so if they encounter Arabic people, they would know if they have to stretch their hand when greeting women or not, and that would be for religious reasons."

Addressing Cultural Learning Challenges

TA, TB, and TC explained that one of the challenges they still encounter with first-level Arabic language learners is trying to understand the many subcultures within the Arab world. Those students, TB stated, come "from different backgrounds" despite the fact that they are American-born and "so they adapt themselves to that American culture more than the Arabic culture. They find that there is a struggle between the two." However, one thing TB does to alleviate this problem is find "a common ground between both cultures." Similarly, TC stated:

> I have students who are basically not in touch with their culture, students who try to live their culture, and students who are in between and, therefore, I always have to struggle to challenge the three levels, if not more, in the same classroom.

Interestingly, TD finds it quite challenging, though enjoyable, to discuss any cultural aspect in the classroom. TD also mentioned that when a cultural issue emerges during reading a literary selection, he/she and the students "talk about this culturally." Similarly, TC asserted that discussing cultural aspects "is the best part of the lesson." TD mentioned that when a cultural issue emerges during reading a literary selection, he/she and the students "talk about this culturally." On the other hand, TE thought it is quite challenging to deliver a lesson without appropriate linguistic and cultural resources. She said, "The lack of materials in general in the market that you need always of other cultures and languages" in turn forces teachers of Arabic "to depend on themselves producing and preparing" the materials.

Moreover, TA and TB thought that cultural awareness in first-level Arabic language classes can be achieved when culture is perceived not as a luxury but an integral component of the Arabic language. Thus, one way to achieve this goal, TA believed, besides finding the right materials and resources, is to get professional "training that focuses on culture." TB mentioned that some teachers in general believe "that culture should go side-by-side with the teaching of language" and that it is necessary to cooperate "between the house and the teacher; the students and home, as well as the school in order to enhance the teaching of Arabic culture." TB said, "If the teacher is not well prepared, how could he/she teach those learners [for whom] Arabic is a second language to them?" This, he continued, is "the duty of the school district to prepare Arabic teachers." On the other hand, TD was not quite sure if cultural learning can be achieved in first-level Arabic language classes because of budget problems. TD said, "It would be wonderful if we can take them overseas to the country where they can really interact with other people directly." For TC, the teaching of culture is "part of the language" itself and that is why it must "be connected to the cultural aspect of the language." Hence, daily practice of the culture, differentiating instruction, and "showing the uniqueness of every culture and every language" are essential in promoting the teaching and learning of Arabic culture. TD also emphasized that through daily practice and discussion of various aspects of culture, teachers of Arabic may be able to enhance first-level learners' cultural skills. TD thought it is unfortunate that some schools still treat culture as an add-on, but he/she also stressed that teaching culture is intertwined with teaching language.

> In some schools and in some colleges, the time is very limited and the program is very intensive. It is full of exercises, like, many chapters you have to cover in the book. They hardly give you time, like, any moment to talk about cultural awareness to the students, unfortunately, but in [city name deleted], in our program, it is a necessity. It is part of our program. It has to be there. (TD)

Similarly, TE thought that culture must never be treated as a luxury but as "an integrated component of the language. It is an essential component of the language and the one that makes it alive, that gives life to the language." However, she emphasized that cultural awareness can be achieved in first-level Arabic language classes if teachers "involve students in the process" especially when learners "go research things and come to class to discuss it."

Evidence of Quality

The interview questions were generated to seek Arab American high school teachers' perceptions regarding developing cultural awareness in first-level Arabic language classes. Three themes and six subthemes surfaced from the interview recordings and transcriptions, and the teacher's field notes regarding nonverbal language and expressions were documented. Only we knew the names of the teachers who voluntarily participated in the research study and the names of the two sites where the study took place.

In this study, we utilized rich, thick descriptions, as well as two of the most common but essential strategies to reach internal validity: member checks—taking the preliminary findings back to the participants who were interviewed to determine accuracy of transcriptions—and peer review—asking a doctoral candidate who is very familiar with this research study to assess whether the findings are credible and believable based on the data gathered (Merriam & Associates, 2002).Hatch (2002) defined *member checking* as the process of giving participants an opportunity "to react to tentative findings generated by the researcher" (p. 101). Before the interview transcripts were formally coded and analyzed, we used member checking as a technique to improve the rigor of this research study. At the conclusion of each interview, participants were informed that a copy of the interview transcript would be sent to them for the purpose of correcting errors, commenting, checking for consistency, and asserting that the initial interpretations were correct (Rubin & Rubin, 2005). They were also asked to send it back within two days via inter-school mail with comments and/or necessary changes. Prolonged discussion with the teachers over the phone followed to ensure that their comments were interpreted as intended. In addition, we scheduled a single debriefing meeting to detect biases and assumptions, clarify vague descriptions, as well as ensure credibility and validity "so that the account will resonate with people other than the researcher" (Creswell, 2003, p. 196). To avoid biases, no controversial issues were discussed and no personal values about any teacher were directly or indirectly disseminated. Finally, hard copies of the transcripts and cassettes of the taped interviews were kept locked in a file cabinet for protection.

Conclusion

The purpose of this research study was to investigate the development of cultural awareness of first-level Arabic language learners. Data collection and analysis made use of information gathered solely from individual interviews of five high school teachers of Arabic. The research study was methodologically guided by a qualitative case study design. The primary question and two subquestions were designed to guide the one-on-one semistructured interviews with the high school teachers of Arabic. The analysis and interpretation of the interviews resulted in three major themes and six subthemes. Individual themes and corresponding quotes were also noted (Appendix D). The emergent themes revealed that developing cultural awareness of first-level Arabic language learners can be achieved when language is intertwined with that of culture and when the practices, products, and perspectives of culture are interwoven. Leijuan and Zhihong (2011) noted that "language and culture are intimately related. Language is both the carrier and main manifestation of culture" (p. 279). Findings also indicated that developing cultural awareness can be achieved through practicing culture in and beyond the school setting and through dealing with the persistent and "profound challenges" (Yuanfang & Bing, 2009, p. 457) encountered in class when teaching the cultural component of the language. Thus, past or current experiences of teachers of first-level Arabic language learners may affect future experiences when teaching cultural awareness since the content of culture plays an important role when a foreign language is taught (Zhu, 2010).

Chapter Five discusses the results of the research study and its implications. It also offers recommendations for future study.

CHAPTER FIVE
DISCUSSION AND
RECOMMENDATIONS

Overview of the Study

In this qualitative case study, we examined perceptions of Arab American high school teachers of Arabic regarding developing cultural awareness in first-level Arabic language classes. Chapter Five analyzes the findings of the study as they relate to the research questions. It also summarizes the purpose of the study, reviews the methodology utilized, discusses the significance of the three major themes and six subthemes that emerged, explores several areas of strength and limitations, offers recommendations for possible future research, and concludes with a brief summary.

Following the tragic events of September 11, 2001, the need to master foreign languages and cultures has become "increasingly critical for the nation's security and its ability to compete in the global marketplace" (Jackson & Malone, 2009, p. 5). This critical needled to the increase of K–12 Arabic language enrollment in U.S. schools especially when the learning standards for foreign language learning, known as the five Cs—**communication**, cultures, connections, comparisons, and communities—were endorsed (National Standards, 2006). Although previous literature supported intertwining language and culture in foreign language classrooms in the United States, there was no significant guidance on how teachers of Arabic could develop students' **cultural awareness through** incorporating the practices, products, and perspectives of the Arabic culture.

For this research study, five Arab American high school teachers of Arabic at two high schools were recruited through my personal e-mail account to get their approval to be interviewed by the researchers. The purpose behind conducting semi-structured interviews with the teachers was to understand how the three aspects of culture—**practices, products, and perspectives**—were incorporated and what best instructional practices, cultural resources, and teaching methodologies were being implemented and represented in the first-level Arabic language classrooms. The interviews were tape recorded and accompanied by field notes. Three major themes and six subthemes emerged as a result of the interview transcripts, field notes, and review of the existing literature.

The purpose of this casestudy research was to investigate Arab American high school teachers' perceptions regarding developing cultural awareness in first-level Arabic language classes. This qualitative research study provided a review of the literature regarding Arabic language teaching, the standards for learning Arabic as a world language, and the standard of culture in the National Standards for foreign language learning. For the purpose of this study, we pursued answers to the following primary research question and two sub-questions:

- How do Arabic language teachers develop Arabic cultural awareness in first-level high school Arab language learners?
    1. What are Arabic language teachers' perceptions regarding the inclusion of cultural awareness in first-level Arabic language classes?
    2. What cultural activities do Arabic language teachers implement in an effort to generate cultural awareness in first-level Arab language classes?

Interpretation of the Findings

The purpose of this qualitative research study was to investigate Arab American high school teachers' perceptions regarding developing cultural awareness of first-level Arabic language learners. A qualitative casestudy design was adopted since the focus was on the teachers' various perspectives and current or past experiences regarding the inclusion of culture in their beginning Arabic classes. Data were collected solely from one-on-one interviews of five high school teachers of Arabic. Data from the teachers' individual interviews were then analyzed and interpreted for recurrent themes. This research study resulted in three major themes and six subthemes. The emergent themes revealed that developing cultural awareness in first-level Arabic language classes is possible and can be achieved when teaching of Arabic language is intertwined with its culture and when the practices, products, and perspectives of culture are interwoven.

In the course of world language instruction, Ömer and Ali (2011) asserted that when people communicate with each other, they use verbal and nonverbal language to express their thoughts and feelings.

> As a society's language and cultural values of that society have similar characteristics, every language should reflect the culture of the society in which the language is spoken, and reversely every culture should contain linguistic figures. This can be thought [of] as a chicken–egg question which could not be answered yet and also would not be answered forever (Ömer& Ali, 2011, p. 257).

Ping (2010), however, believed that although language and culture must not be taught as separate entities in language classes, language learners may not be able to develop their cultural skills before the target language is learned. The researcher said:

> Foreign language classes where students do not learn to communicate in the target language are the functional equivalent of reading classes where students do no learn to read, writing classes where students do not learn to write, and mathematics classes where students do not learn to add, subtract, multiply, or divide (Ping, 2010, p. 560).

The inclusion of culture in first-level Arabic language classes was supported and based on Vygotsky's (1929, 1978) sociocultural theory and Gardner's (1985, 2001, 2006) socioeducational theory. Language learners are social beings; therefore, using the target language when communicating with other speakers is a must to belong to that linguistic community. Thus, to attain the goal of learning Arabic as a world language, teachers of Arabic must be able to create a positive cultural learning student-centered environment so learners become highly motivated to learn the Arabic language and culture and become part of the host group.

Theme 1: Connecting Language and Culture

The recurrent theme of connecting language and culture was evidenced through the individual teachers' responses to the interview questions. In defining *culture*, all five teachers had a common vision of it and how purposeful and critical it is to integrate culture especially in the first-level Arabic language classroom. Côté, Simard, Falardeau, Emery-Bruneau, and Carrier (2010) stated that "culture is not limited to a single meaning; it is composed of all patterns of significance that humans create to make meaning of their lives" (p. 33).

In spite of the teachers' unanimous responses regarding the connection between language and culture, the focus in first-level Arabic language classes is thought to be more on the linguistic aspect than its cultural implications. Furstenberg (2010) reported:

> Even though we always assert that we teach language *and* culture, we tend to focus, at least in beginning and intermediate courses, on language teaching, leaving "culture" at the periphery. The very link between the two remains an elusive abstraction, with the result that language and culture are often divorced from each other (p. 329).

The data analysis presented in Chapter Four showed that teaching Arabic as a world language to first-level learners must take place in a cultural context because language and culture are closely connected. Language and culture must be embedded, as Q. Yi (2010) noted:

> By failing to draw language learners' attention to the cultural elements and to discuss their implication, the teachers allow misconceptions to develop in the students' minds. Mere fluency in utterance in a foreign language without any awareness of their culture implications or of their proper situational use, or the

reading of a material without a realization of the values would certainly lead to a total failure in language learning in any sense of liberal education. (p. 58)

Thus, the teachers further supported the notion that through daily practice, creating cultural situations, and using authentic cultural resources and materials, first-level language learners can become more motivated to learn the target language (Sarıçoban & Çalışkan, 2011). Sarıçoban and Çalışkan(2011) stated:

> The pedagogical separation of language from culture is justified in the sense that language can stand alone. It can be taught without referring to the culture. It does so obviously in literature, and the long association of language and literature teaching has some explanation for the separation. On the other hand, the tendency to treat language quite independently of culture to which it constantly refers cannot be justified; it disregards the nature of language teaching. (p. 10)

Moreover, raising first-level Arabic language learners' **cultural awareness**, which basically deals with enhancing learners' **cultural knowledge and tolerance**, is not only vital but it can also be attained when language teachers implement relevant reading texts, stories, and other literature genres, as Bacha and Bahous (2011) emphasized. This was clearly reflected in the teachers' responses to the interview questions. The researchers noted that one of the important but difficult aspects of teaching culture is how to make learners "respond positively to the literature through which culture is transmitted . . . to see the relevance to their studies or lives" (Bacha & Bahous, 2011, p. 1324). They thought that world language teachers can help their language learners preserve their cultural identity by exposing them to literary works that connect East and West. With this in mind, it was not evident from the teachers' responses if they have utilized literature that bridges East and West.

In addition, there was no evidence from the teachers that cultural awareness can be developed through allowing learners to create their own authentic learning situations and contexts (Nikitina, 2011). Language learners, as Harrison (2009) indicated, must be given ample opportunities to show responsibility for their own cultural learning by selecting, organizing, and utilizing their own cultural topics and research agendas. Even though the teachers' responses to the interview questions revealed incorporating various cultural activities and sources, research shows that teachers can enhance cultural acquisition of the host language by incorporating many more cultural-based language teaching techniques, such as illustrations, videos, interviews, photographs, songs and plays, and fieldwork(Lili, 2011).

Still, recognizing the complexity of teaching culture to first-level Arabic language learners, as the data analysis presented in Chapter Four and the aforementioned themes revealed, is crucial in cultural acquisition. Lili (2011) stated:

> Language learning is a complex phenomenon with different variables concerning the social-cultural elements of the contexts, an interactional approach can ensure that a social perspective of second language development and instruction contributes to having a positive effect on the nature and quality of language

learning, which activates the autonomous learning motivation and creates diversity in the learning atmosphere(p. 1033).

Theme 2: Developing Culture Learning

Harrison (2009) explained that the various approaches utilized to teach the target culture have not been well matched with effective methods or tools of assessment. The five teachers revealed that they, like so many other world language teachers, normally assess their students' linguistic and cultural skills, such as grammar and vocabulary skills, by giving them fill-in-the-blank activities, true/false statements, and multiple-choice questions; however, as Arens (2010) emphasized, language teachers have not been well prepared to assess students' cultural skills, and noted:

> Traditionally, students have been assessed on the basis of a finished product, whether it was a paper, an exam, or a project. However, because the focus is now on a process of discovering, the question arises: "How does one assess process?" I will not dwell on that topic except to say that new modes and tools are required to aptly assess what students have learned and understood as they went along their journey. Portfolios and reflection logbooks are appropriate tools. (p. 331)

In broad terms, the practices, products, and the perspectives of culture, as Muir (2007) reported, can be divided into
1. High culture, including politics, philosophy, education, literature, art
2. Deep culture, including sense of value, mode of thinking, code of conduct, religious beliefs, criterion of morality
3. Popular culture, including the patterns of customs, ceremony and propriety of social contact, way of life, family patterns, and even concrete catering culture, tea culture (p. 38).

In this research study, the interviewed teachers experienced some level of frustration in the area of assessing their first-level Arabic language learners' cultural learning. Nevertheless, this frustration seems to have been shared with other world language teachers as well. Schulz and Ganz (2010) reported that one of the teachers who participated in a research on the teaching of culture summarized her frustration as follows:

> People keep asking me to test culture and no one seems able to tell me exactly what they mean by that. I always say, everything we do is culture. But evidently, that is not what is meant. So I wish there were a template, because my understanding of including culture in a test is evidently not the same as whatever assessment people are asking for (p. 181).

Theme 3: Improving Culture Learning and Teaching

According to Gocer (2010), culture learning and teaching can be improved not only through creating a positive cultural learning environment but also through responsive and meaningful communication with students and parents. Nevertheless, the desire to build effective communication with parents or other community stakeholders was not evident in one of this study's teacher's responses during the interview. Gocer (2010) emphasized that "teachers who make a good communication with their students; prepare their materials to be used beforehand; and act more professionally in determining the strategies, methods and techniques to be used are the ones who can perform their occupations consciously" (p. 196).

There must always be room for improving culture learning and teaching in first-level Arabic language classes. The practices, products, and perspectives of culture must never be taught in isolation regardless of what level of Arabic is being taught, a position reflected in the standards of teaching Arabic as a foreign language (National Standards, 2006) but not adopted, according to the teachers' responses to the interview questions. Throughout their individual interviews, the teachers were able to list a few general cultural themes/topics, such as foods, that they have utilized on culture days; however, they did not offer details as to how that specific element of culture is incorporated in their first-level Arabic language classes. There was little emphasis, if any, on how to deal with specific vocabulary and practices associated with eating at an Arabic restaurant, for example. According to Byram (2011), the concept of the perspective of culture must be connected and interwoven with the practices and products of the target language. Hence, world language teachers must be able to utilize the perspective of culture in beginning language classes to develop students' cultural skills and competency. Byram (2011) also called for language teachers to write lesson plans that link the linguistic with the cultural and personal perspectives:

> The goals of this cultural lesson for instance [are] threefold: [a] students review, practice, pronouns; [b] students are introduced to and use vocabulary and practices associated with eating in a restaurant; and [c] students learn about and reflect on the use of politeness strategies (p. 531).

Similarly, Cutshall (2012) strongly advised language educators to:

> Realize that following a textbook and reading over the cultural points that in the occasional sidebar is not sufficient to impart cultural knowledge to their students.
> Nor is it enough to offer 'Cultural Fridays' or to think culture is taken care of by celebrating a holiday, learning a few dances, or tasting some authentic food now and then (p. 33).

Implications for Social Change

In this research study, the data indicated that developing cultural awareness in first-level Arabic language classes is not only possible but rather necessary beyond national security and global economic challenges. In addition, the results of this study can be utilized, even at the local level, to inform K–12 world language teachers in general and Arabic teachers in particular as to the importance of harmonizing language and culture through incorporating the practices, products, and perspectives of culture especially in beginning language classes. Jackson and Malone (2009) stated that global communication is part of every daily routine and

> Businesses that are able to interact with customers in their own languages build strong ties to their communities as well as loyalty among their customers. To continue to compete successfully in this environment, all Americans should have basic functional knowledge of a foreign language and culture (p. 3).

Similarly, Su (2008) stressed that because "language is a part of culture and culture is a part of language" (pp. 377–78), he always emphasizes to his language students the importance of not only demonstrating awareness of the practices, products, and perspectives of the language learned but also making every effort to actually "communicate with others beyond the school and home settings" (p. 378), and that is the heart of sociocultural perspective. Hence, the teaching of Arabic culture seems to have been and still is a priority in first-level Arabic language classes where the five interviewed teachers teach; however, as Byrnes (2010) emphasized, "the cultural dimension of foreign language teaching needs to fulfill purposes that are both educational and utilitarian" (p. 320). With the Arabic *Standards* in place, it would be worthwhile for Arabic language teachers and educators to collaborate so the Arabic language program continues to advance in the overall teaching and learning of Arabic culture.

Moreover, teachers at all Arabic levels may be able to use the findings of this study to collaborate to employ and share common best cultural practices and assessment tools, as well as pedagogical student-centered strategies. With proper certification, adequate training, and expertise, learning of Arabic at the beginning, intermediate, or advanced level becomes not only successful but also a rewarding experience for teachers and students equally.

Perhaps the ultimate outcome of this researcher study is preparing us as world language teachers to reexamine our own teaching of the three Ps of culture at all levels of Arabic language instruction. Despite the fact that it may be quite impossible to balance between the linguistic and cultural features of Arabic study, overcoming barriers to integrating the three Ps into Arabic language curriculum is a must. This can be accomplished through dedicated collaboration among teachers of Arabic and unlimited professional development opportunities based on best cultural practices. Teachers of Arabic have the potential to expand student learning and their own teaching methods of the language and its culture by making important contributions to the language program. Without the teachers' collegiality, novice teachers of Arabic will be deprived of the good training, necessary cultural resources, and peer coaching they are entitled to be provided with. The study provides a good starting point for world language educators for reviewing the entire K–12 Arabic language program through the perspectives of Arabic learners themselves and by a cultural approach in teaching the Arabic language.

Hence, positive social change includes making a paradigm change in Arabic language instruction for teachers and learners alike as learning of the Arabic language becomes more culture centered. Teachers of Arabic language and culture will be free of inherent bias caused by their own cultural perceptions and beliefs.

This will create better understanding and appreciation of the culture of the language they are teaching, thus allowing learners of Arabic a learning experience focused on cultural competency and cross-cultural understanding. This satisfies the need for global communication necessitated by the rapidly shrinking boundaries between various cultures.

Recommendations for Action

This study of the perceptions of Arab American high school teachers of Arabic regarding developing cultural awareness in first-level Arabic language classes provided insights to better understand learners' **cultural needs and teachers'** challenges. Teachers of Arabic at the elementary and secondary levels should pay close attention to the findings of this research study as they can serve as a valuable guide to understanding the significance of utilizing effective cultural tools and responding to learners' **cultural needs.**

Also, the findings of the research study stress the urgency of expanding learners' linguistic and cultural knowledge through utilizing technology in world language classes. Experimenting with a wide range of computer applications, such as word processing, e-mail, chat, PowerPoint and the Internet, will not only enhance mastery of the Arabic keyboard or composition with fewer errors in MSA, but also help learners advance their cultural and communication skills through sending and receiving e-mails in Arabic (Madhany, 2007). Equally important, getting acquainted with computer applications can be a valuable tool for novice teachers; it can improve their instruction by providing them with the right syllabi and lesson plans written by more experienced teachers of Arabic. Al-Batal and Belnap(2006) stated that "the right combination of technology and human interaction has the potential to significantly expand student learning opportunities" (p. 399).

Moreover, there is an immediate urgency for teachers of Arabic as a world language to apply research–best cultural practices especially for beginning classes and to be consistent in delivering and assessing the right cultural activities and skills. Jackson and Malone (2009) emphasized that "for students to learn foreign languages and cultures, trained teachers and high-quality instructional materials and assessments are critical" (p. 6). This requires teachers of Arabic and other world language leaders and educators to participate in training workshops and seminars that focus on applying the five Cs—communication, cultures, comparisons, connections, and communities—and aligning the three Ps—practices, products, and perspectives—with topics/themes taught in class.

Since this research study presented only a snapshot of the teachers' **teaching** of culture to first-level Arabic language learners, further recommendations for action include
1. Teachers' weekly meetings/planning time with other K–12 teachers in which Arabic language teaching takes place. This can be a very powerful, collaborative, and collegial opportunity to ensure meaningful learning on how to use cultural assessment methodologies appropriately.

2. Encourage teachers of Arabic to observe each other's classroom instruction (at least twice a month) to try new instructional strategies on best learning practices and techniques. This encouragement should happen within and across the schools in the district. Alosh, Elkhafaifi, and Hammoud (2006) stated that a native speaker of Arabic does not necessarily make a competent teacher because he or she "may not be able to demonstrate an awareness of [the] minimum level of teaching standards to meet the expectations of students, parents, and society" (p. 410).
3. Ensure quality teaching of the language by hiring teachers who are endorsed to teach Arabic as a foreign language and demand certification from those who have the expertise but lack the endorsement. Hence, this kind of profession alism is "perhaps our greatest need, since nearly half of all Arabic teachers receive little or no training in foreign language pedagogy" (Al-Batal & Belnap, 2006, p. 392).
4. A summary and synopsis of the findings of the current research study will be disclosed to the two high school principals and five teachers of Arabic to see how they can improve the learning and teaching of Arabic language and culture in their beginning, intermediate, and advanced Arabic classes.

Limitations

The purpose of this qualitative case study was to investigate Arab American high school teachers' perceptions regarding developing cultural awareness of first-level Arabic language learners. As with all studies, this research study has a few limitations. This research may be limited in scope because of the small number of high school teachers, who happen to be the only ones who teach Arabic as a world language in the district where the research study took place. This may be a limiting factor in generalizing findings not only beyond the same school district but also within the sites included in the study due to the exclusion of other world language teachers. Also, the study was a one-time interview-based research. Perhaps conducting nonparticipant observations of the teachers' classes before and after the interviews took place could have added richness for the type of results being sought and more depth to the issue explored.

Investigated solely from the qualitative perspective, this research study allowed a glimpse into how the teachers of Arabic as a world language perceive developing cultural awareness in first-level Arabic language learners. Had a mixed-method approach been conducted, a more impressive array of major themes could have emerged. Finally, developing cultural awareness in first-level Arabic language classes requires thorough analysis of the materials, methodology, and curriculum implemented; however, since those issues were not explored as such, an additional set of limitations should be considered.

Recommendations for Further Study

Due to the limited number of Arab American high school teachers of Arabic in the district where the research study took place, more research is recommended regarding the inclusion of Arabic culture and the teachers' and the learners' cultural needs at the elementary, intermediate, and high school level. The recommended lines of research must be directed to reflect on the teaching of culture to first-level Arabic language learners at all school levels. Also, with sufficient participation of second-generation Arabic language learners at the secondary level, future studies can further emerge to compare and contrast their perceptions regarding developing cultural awareness with the teachers.

Furthermore, more quantitative research needs to be conducted in the elementary schools of this study's district where Arabic is taught as a world language to survey students to determine if the teaching of the language continues to reflect the five Cs "in a systematically articulated approach at the middle and high school levels" (Jackson & Malone, 2009, p. 6).

In recognition of the significance and importance of integrating culture learning into first-level Arabic language classes, further mixed-method studies are recommended surveying K–12 teachers of Arabic district-wide, investigating current assessment best practices and sharing actual assessment practices and tools with first-level Arabic language learners. The assessment tools may address crucial components, such as listening, reading, speaking, writing, and cultural literacy skills, to determine if the district-developed assessment rubrics are in compliance with credit award criteria as determined by the Michigan Department of Education.

In today's global world, for more effective instruction, teachers of Arabic as a world language need the necessary skills in utilizing technology in the Arabic language classroom. With that in mind, more research must be conducted to determine learners' capabilities of developing and enhancing their language acquisition and cultural literacy through student-to-student e-mail, chat, PowerPoint, word processing, as well as web-based research.

In addition, further research is highly recommended to measure the affective factors of first-level Arabic language learners, such as their beliefs, motives, and attitudes toward Arabic language and culture learning. Understanding learners' overall affective abilities, motivations, and attitudes toward learning the language may help teachers redirect their teaching, especially after detecting the problems and real challenges as learning of the language takes place.

Finally, further research examining the treatment of culture in the high school textbooks that are accredited by public and charter schools within the same school district where this research study took place is highly recommended in order "to investigate what aspects of culture learning/teaching" (K. Lee, 2009, p. 92) are included and what cultural domain is addressed.

Reflection on the Researcher's Experience

Perhaps one of the most positive effects of this research study was that it gave our colleagues ample opportunity to reflect on their teaching—present and past practices—which is a characteristic that distinguishes them from novice teachers. This reflective approach on the part of the teachers shows how committed they have been and still are to their job as teachers of Arabic and how aware they are of their students' linguistic and cultural needs, which in turn results in heightening and enhancing their students' motivation to the learning of culture. In fact, "many of our students will not have much cause to use the L2 after they finish requirements and so what they are most likely to remember two or ten years hence is not grammar or vocabulary but some aspects of cultural identity" (Arens, 2010, p. 322).

Still, learning for teachers of Arabic cannot stop once the expertise or motivation begins; the truth of the matter is that the ability to teach a world language consists of "knowledge, skills, and practice. Skills come from applying knowledge to the classroom. And practice in teaching is guided by a carefully designed program in ongoing, reflective practice" (England, 2006, p. 420). With that in mind, we were quite surprised at one of the participants' lack of knowledge of the five Cs—communication, cultures, connections, comparisons, and communities—during the interview. In fact, the participant asked me to stop recording on that day and to resume the next day in an attempt to learn about the five Cs. That honesty on the part of that teacher was a source of joy and pride for us; the current research study heightened his awareness and positively influenced his teaching behavior.

Even though all the participants described directly what cultural skills and activities have been incorporated in their first-level Arabic language classes, we were not sure if they actually knew what the three Ps—practices, products, and perspectives—are, and how much of Arabic culture has been included. Byrd, Hlas, Watzke, and Valencia (2011) stated that "it is not surprising that due to minimum coverage of culture in teacher education programs; teachers may lack the background knowledge that can connect practices and products to perspectives" (p. 9). Thus, teaching cultural skills remains problematic and challenging for world language teachers especially when they try to evaluate and assess their students' cultural skills. Hence, our colleagues (the participants) are often "left to their own devices to find cultural resources, instructional strategies, and frameworks for the teaching of culture" (Byrd et al., 2011, p. 5).

Furthermore, this research study has helped us understand the complexities of teaching and assessing culture in its three components—*practices, products, and perspectives*. This study in itself has helped me realize that the number of years students may spend learning Arabic language does not necessarily guarantee their competency in the culture of the language. The results of this research study identified *perspectives* as the most complicated cultural dimension to teach. We came to realize that it is vital to provide my colleagues with the support needed to broaden their understanding of this cultural aspect and to advance their knowledge of all cultural resources. We believed that strengthening the instruction of all three aspects of culture is critical especially if we strive to motivate students in learning the language. There was a growing awareness of my own beliefs regarding how much effort has been involved in my teaching of the cultural *practices, products, and perspectives* of the Arabic culture.

Finally, we hope that this research study stimulates, among all teachers of Arabic, more discussion regarding the role Arabic language ought to play in developing cultural awareness and literacy in first-level Arabic language classes, for the "challenge ahead is to develop teacher preparation programs, and instructional curricula materials, and assessments that reflect that stance" (Schulz & Ganz, 2010, p. 190).

Conclusion

The purpose of this research study was to investigate the perceptions of Arab American high school teachers of Arabic regarding developing cultural awareness in first-level Arab language classes. Recently, foreign language instruction has gone beyond the occasional inclusion of facts about the history or civilization of a specific target culture; the emphasis nowadays is on the language's social characteristics and on how language and culture can be integrated to promote the language learner's ability to communicate with others who come from various linguistic and cultural backgrounds (Larzen-Ostermark, 2009; Ömer & Ali, 2011).

The results of this study support the notion that "learning of language is a complex process that goes beyond acquiring grammar and vocabulary and being able to engage in oral and written communication" (Altstaedter & Jones, 2009, p. 64); that "the grammar instruction is not sufficient but should be complemented with authentic communication" (Ganjabi, 2011, p. 47); that the inclusion of Arabic culture is critical in language instruction; and that teachers need a high level of expertise, training, professional competence as well as availability of cultural resources "for keeping up-to-date with their profession" (England, 2006, p. 431).

In this research study, the teachers were able to articulate the ways in which they teach and implement the cultural aspects of the Arabic language in their first-level Arabic language classes. Though each one of the participants has his or her unique way of teaching Arabic culture, they all see the connection between language and culture, the need to carefully create and design appropriate assessment cultural tools, as well as understanding the complexities and challenges they face, on a daily basis, as they try to help their learners become integratively motivated to learn the language through culture. Huang (2011) stated:

> Language is a carrier of the culture. Any kind of existing language implies the cultural intention of the people who use this kind of language in the course of long-term historical development. Only when one acquaints himself with those imply in the cultural intension behind this kind of language, can he return the flesh and blood of the language and comprehend the concrete meaning of the cultural issues (p. 248).

The emergence of the standards for Arabic language learning (the five Cs)—communication, cultures, connections, comparisons, and communities—as well as the three aspects of culture—practices, products, and perspectives—

> necessitates an urgent call for change with regard to the place of culture in the Arabic language curriculum. Arabic material developers and language coordinators should be encouraged to regard culture as an integral co-curricular component... cultural knowledge should be considered a priority over linguistic knowledge in the classroom(Abdalla, 2006, p. 325).

Leijuan and Zhihong (2011) stated that "culture in language learning is also an essential part of knowledge that should be included along with rather than an extended skill to the teaching of listening, speaking, reading, and writing" (p. 280). Culture is the heart of all effective communication. In fact, as long as languages exist, there will always be cultures (Izadpanah, 2011). However, it remains an absolute challenge for world language teachers in general to link the three pieces of culture together rather than slicing culture into three separate entities—practices, products, and perspectives—in any given language curriculum.

REFERENCES

Abdalla, M. (2006). Arabic immersion and summer programs in the United States. In K. Wahba, Z. Taha, & L. England (Eds.), *Handbook for Arabic language teaching professionals in the 21st century* (pp. 317–330). Mahwah, NJ: Erlbaum.

Ajayi, L. (2008). ESL theory–practice dynamics: The difficulty of integrating sociocultural perspectives into pedagogical practices. *Foreign Language Annals, 41*(4), 639–659.

Al-Batal, M. (2007). Perspectives: Arabic and national language educational policy. *Modern Language Journal, 91*(2), 268–271.

Al-Batal, M., & Belnap, K. (2006). The teaching and learning of Arabic in the United States: Realities, needs, and future directions. In K. Wahba, Z. Taha, & L. England (Eds.), *Handbook for Arabic language and teaching professionals in the 21st century* (pp. 389–399). Mahwah, NJ: Erlbaum.

Allen, R. (2007). Arabic-flavor of the moment: Whence, why, and how? *Modern Language Journal, 91*(2), 258–261. doi:10.111/j.1540-4781.2007.00543_6x

Alosh, M., Elkhafaifi, H., & Hammoud, S.D. (2006). Professional standards for teachers of Arabic. In K. Wahba, Z. Taha, & L. England (Eds.), *Handbook for Arabic language and teaching professionals in the 21st century* (pp. 409–418). Mahwah, NJ: Erlbaum.

Altstaedter, L., & Jones, B. (2009).Motivating students' foreign language and culture acquisition through web-based inquiry. *Foreign Language Annals, 42*(4), 640–657. doi:10.1111/j.1944-9720.2009.01047.x

Arab American Institute Foundation. (2010). Retrieved from http://www.aaiusa. or/arab-americans/22/demographics.

ArabBay.com. (2001). *The Arab world.* Retrieved from http://www.arabbay.com /arabmap. htm.

Arens, K. (2010). The field of culture: The standards as a model for teaching culture. *Modern Language Journal, 94*(2), 321–324. doi:10.1111/j.1540-4781.2010.01025.x

Askham, P. (2008). Context and identity: Exploring adult learners' experiences of higher education. *Journal of Further and Higher Education, 32*(1), 85–97.

Axelon, B. (2006). The future of foreign languages: In an increasingly competitive and open world, the demand for language instruction in Chinese and Arabic is rising. Don't let your students miss out. *Scholastic Administrator, 6*(3) 42–45.

Ayouby, K. K. (2004). *Speak American! or language, power and education in Dearborn, Michigan: A case study of Arabic heritage learners and their community.* Unpublished doctoral dissertation, Nelson Mandela Metropolitan University, Port Elizabeth, South Africa.

Babler, A. (2006). Creating interactive web-based Arabic teaching materials with authoring systems. In K. Wahba, Z. Taha, & L. England (Eds.), *Handbook for Arabic language teaching professionals in the 21st century* (pp. 275–294). Mahwah, NJ: Erlbaum.

Bacha, N., & Bahous, R. (2011). Foreign language education in Lebanon: A context of cultural and curricular complexities. *Journal of Language Teaching & Research, 2*(6), 1320–1328. doi:10.4304/jltr.2.6.1320-1328.

Bakkar, A. (2008). Who says what on the Arabic Internet? Notes about content of Arabic Internet messages. *Journal of Website Promotion, 3*(½), 2–13. doi:10.1080/15533610802052530.

Bartlett, L. (2005). Identity work and cultural artifacts in literacy learning and use: A sociocultural analysis. *Language & Education: An International Journal, 19*(1), 1–9.

Bartoshesky, A. (2003). Teaching culture to foreign language learners. Highlights from the NCLRC 2003 Summer Institute.

Bateman, B. E. (2008). Student teachers' attitudes and beliefs about using the target language in the classroom. *Foreign Language Annals, 41*(1), 11–28.

Belnap, K. (2006). A profile of students of Arabic in U.S. universities. In K. Wahba, Z. Taha, & L. England (Eds.), *Handbook for Arabic language and teaching professionals in the 21st century* (pp. 169–178). Mahwah, NJ: Erlbaum.

Black, L. (2007). Interactive whole class teaching and pupil learning: Theoretical and practical implications. *Language & Education: An International Journal, 21*(4), 271–283.

Bloom, M. (2008). From the classroom to the community: Building cultural awareness in first semester Spanish. *Language, Culture & Curriculum, 21*(2), 103–119. doi:10.2167/lcc349.0.

Bollag, B. (2008). Foreign language departments bring everyday texts to teaching. *Education Digest, 73*(5), 54–58.

Brown, A. V. (2009). Less commonly taught language and commonly taught language students: A demographic and academic comparison. *Foreign Language Annals, 42*(3), 405–423.

Brown, K., & Kraehe, A. (2010). The complexities of teaching the complex: Examining how future educators construct understandings of sociocultural knowledge and schooling. *Educational Studies, 46*(1), 91–115. doi:10.1080/00131940903480175.

Byram, K. A. (2011). Using the concept of perspective to integrate cultural, communicative, and form-focused language instruction. *Foreign Language Annals, 44*(3), 525–543. doi:10.1111/j.1944-9720.2011.01145.x

Byrd, D. R., Hlas, A., Watzke, J., & Valencia, M. (2011). An examination of culture knowledge: A study of L2 teachers' and teacher educators' beliefs and practices. *Foreign Language Annals, 44*(1), 4–39. doi:10.1111/j.1944-9720.2011.01117.x

Byrnes, H. (2010). Revisiting the role of culture in the foreign language curriculum. *Modern Language Journal, 94*(2), 315–317. doi:10.1111/j.1540-4781.2010.01023.x

Chami-Sather, G., & Kretschmer, R., Jr. (2005). Lebanese/Arabic and American children's discourse in group-solving situations. *Language & Education: An International Journal, 19*(1), 10–31.

Christ, T., & Makarani, S. (2009). Teachers' attitudes about teaching English in India: An embedded mixed methods study. *International Journal of Multiple Research Approaches, 3*(1), 73–87.

Coleman, M., & Briggs, R. (2006). *Research methods in educational leadership and management* (6th ed.). Thousand Oaks, CA: Sage.

Comanaru, R., & Noels, K. A. (2009). Self-determination of Chinese as a heritage language. *Canadian Modern Language Review, 66*(1), 131–158. doi:10.3138/cml.131

Côté, H., Simard, D., Falardeau, E., Emery-Bruneau, J., & Carrier, L. (2010). Relation to culture and cultural education on students in high school French-as-a-first-language courses. *Alberta Journal of Educational Research, 56*(1), 31–43.

Creswell, J. W. (1998). *Qualitative inquiry and research design: Choosing among five traditions.* Thousand Oaks, CA: Sage.

Creswell, J. W. (2003). *Research design: Qualitative, quantitative, and mixed methods approaches* (2nd ed.). Thousand Oaks, CA: Sage.

Creswell, J. W. (2005). *Educational research: Planning, conducting, and evaluating quantitative and qualitative research* (2nd ed.). Upper Saddle River, NJ: Pearson.

Creswell, J. W. (2007). *Qualitative inquiry and research design: Choosing among five approaches* (2nd ed.). Thousand Oaks, CA:Sage.

Creswell, J. W. (2009). *Research design:Qualitative, quantitative, and mixed methods approaches* (3rd ed.). Thousand Oaks, CA: Sage.

Csizér, K., & Dörnyei, Z. (2005).The internal structure of language learning motivation and its relationship with language choice and learning effort. *Modern Language Journal, 89*(1), 19–36.

Cutshall, S. (2005). Why we need "the year of languages": Educating language learners. *Language Educator, 62*(4), 20–23.

Cutshall, S. (2007).Riding the wave: Interest in Arabic language learning. *Language Educator, 2*(3), 32–37.

Cutshall, S, (2012). More than a decade of standards: Integrating "Cultures" in your language instruction. *Language Educator, 7*(3), 32-37.

De la O López Abeledo, M. (2008). Sociocultural theory and the genesis of second language development. *Language & Education: An International Journal, 22*(2), 178–181. doi:10.2167/le127b.0

DeSanto, R. (2009). SLA reflections on learning Arabic via a collaborative diary study. *International Journal of Learning, 15*(10), 197–205.

Dewaele, J. (2008). "Appropriateness" in foreign language acquisition and use: Some theoretical, methodological and ethical considerations. *International Review of Applied Linguistics in Language Teaching, 46*(3), 245–265. doi:10.1515/IRAL.2008.011

Duffy, M., & Chenail, R. (2008).Values in qualitative and quantitative research. *Counseling and Values, 53*(1), 22–38.

England, L. (2006). Methodology in Arabic language teacher education. In K. Wahba, Z. Taha, & L. England (Eds.), *Handbook for Arabic language and teaching professionals in the 21st century* (pp. 419–436). Mahwah, NJ: Erlbaum.

Eun, B., & Lim, H.-S. (2009). A sociocultural view of language learning: The importance of meaning-based instruction. *TESL Canada Journal, 27*(1), 13–26.

Extra, G., & Yagmur, K. (2010). Language proficiency and socio-cultural orientation of Turkish and Moroccan youngsters in the Netherlands. *Language & Education: An International Journal, 24*(2), 117–132. doi:10.1080/09500780903096561

Fact Monster.(2012). *Most widely spoken languages in the world.* Retrieved from http://www.factmonster.com/ipka/A0775272.html.

Firth, A., & Wagner, J. (2007). Second/foreign language learning as a social accomplishment: Elaboration in a reconceptualized SLA. *Modern Language Journal, 91,* 800–819.

Fox, R. K., & Diaz-Greenberg, R. (2006). Culture, multiculturalism, and foreign/world language standards in U.S. teacher preparation programs: Toward a discourse of dissonance. *European Journal of Teacher Education, 29*(3), 401–422.

Friesen, N., Feenberg, A., & Smith, G. (2009). Phenomenology and surveillance studies: Returning to the things themselves. *Information Society, 25,* 84–90. doi:10.1080/01972240802701585

Furstenberg, G. (2010). Making culture the core of the language class: Can it be done? *Modern Language Journal, 94*(2), 329–332. doi:10.1111/j.1540-4781.2010.01027.x

Ganjabi, M. (2011). Effective foreign language teaching: A matter of Iranian students' and teachers' beliefs. *English Language Teaching, 4*(2), 46–54. doi:10.5539/elt.v4n2p46

Gardner, R. C. (1985). *The Attitude/Motivation Test Battery: Technical report.* Canada: University of Western Ontario, Department of Psychology.

Gardner, R. C. (2001). Language learning motivation: The student, the teacher, and the researcher. *Texas Papers in Foreign Language Education, 6*(1), 1–18.

Gardner, R. C. (2006). The socio-educational model of second language acquisition: A research paradigm. *EUROSLA Yearbook, 6,* 237–260.

Gardner, R. C., & Lambert, W. E. (1959).Motivational variables in second-language acquisition. *Canadian Journal of Psychology, 13*(4), 266-272.
Ghenghesh, P. (2010). The motivation of L2 learners: Does it decrease with age? *English Language Teaching, 3*(1), 128-141.
Gocer, A. (2010). A qualitative research on the teaching strategies and class applications of the high school teachers who teach English in Turkey as a foreign language. *Education, 131*(1), 196-219.
Gürür, H., & Uzuner, Y. (2010). A phenomenological analysis of the views on co-teaching applications in the inclusion classroom. *Educational Sciences: Theory & Practice, 10*(1), 311-331.
Harrison, L. (2009). Foreign films in the classroom: Gateway to language and culture. *Journal of College Teaching & Learning, 6*(8), 89-93.
Hatch, J. A. (2002). *Doing qualitative research in education settings.* Albany: State University of New York Press.
Hawkey, K. (2006). Teacher and learner perception of language learning activities. *English Language Teachers Journal, 60*(3), 242-252.
Hsu, T. (2005). Research methods and data analysis procedures used by educational researchers. *International Journal of Research & Method in Education, 28*(2), 109-133.
Huang, Y. (2011). On adding cultural contents to English teaching. *Journal of Language Teaching & Research, 2*(1), 248-250. doi:10.4304/jltr.2.1.248-250
Husseinali, G. (2006). Who is studying Arabic and why: A survey of Arabic students' orientations at a major university. *Foreign Language Annals, 39,* 395-412.
Iwamoto, D., Creswell, J., & Caldwell, L. (2007). Feeling the beat: The meaning of rap music for ethnically diverse Midwestern college students—A phenomenological study. *Adolescence: An International Quarterly Devoted to the Physiological, Psychiatric, Sociological, and Educational Aspects of the Second Decade of Human Life, 42*(166), 337.
Izadpanah, S. (2011). The review study: The place of culture in English language teaching. *US-China Foreign Language, 9*(2), 109-116.
Jackson, F. H., & Malone, M.E. (2009). *Building the foreign language capacity we need: Toward a comprehensive strategy for a national language framework.* Retrieved from http://www.cal.org/resources/languageframework.pdf
Janesick, V. J. (2004). *Stretching exercises for qualitative researchers* (2nd ed.). Thousand Oaks, CA: Sage.
Jenkins, T.S. (2009). A portrait of culture in a contemporary America. *NASPA Journal, 46*(2), 131-162.
Ketchum, E. (2006). The cultural baggage of second language reading: An approach to understanding the practices and perspectives of a nonnative product. *Foreign Language Annals, 39*(1), 22-42.
Kramsch, C. (1985). Classroom interaction and discourse options. *Studies in Second Language Acquisition, 7,* 169-183.
Kramsch, C. (2006). Perspectives: From communicative competence to symbolic competence. *Modern Language Journal, 90,* 249.

Larson, P. (2006). Perspectives: The return of the text: A welcome challenge for less commonly taught languages. *Modern Language Journal, 90*, 255–258.

Larzen-Ostermark, E. (2009). Language teacher education in Finland and the cultural dimension of foreign language teaching—A student teacher perspective. *European Journal of Teacher Education, 32*(4), 401–421. doi:10.1080/02619760903012688

Lee, J. S. (2005). Through the learners' eyes: Reconceptualizing the heritage and non-heritage learner of the less commonly taught languages. *Foreign Language Annals, 38*(4), 554–567.

Lee, K. (2009). Treating culture: What 11 high school EFL conversation textbooks in South Korea do. *English Teaching: Practice & Critique, 8*(1), 76–96.

Lee, S., Butler, M. B., &Tippins, D. J. (2007).A case study of an early childhood teachers' perspective on working with English language learners. *Multicultural Education, 15*(1), 43–49.

Leijuan, H., & Zhihong, L. (2011).Exploring cultural knowledge in EFL teaching in an EAVSC. *Journal of Language Teaching & Research, 2*(1), 279–283. doi:10.4304/jltr.2.1279-283

Levering, B. (2006). Epistemological issues in phenomenological research: How authoritative are people's accounts of their own perceptions. *Journal of Philosophy of Education, 40*(4), 451–464.

Lili, D. (2011). Practical techniques for cultural-based language teaching in the EFL classroom. *Journal of Language Teaching & Research, 2*(5), 1031–1036. doi:10.4304/jltr.2.5.1031-1036

Lim, J. H. (2008). The road not taken: Two African-American girls' experiences with school mathematics. *Race Ethnicity and Education, 11*(3), 303–317.

Lorduy, D., Lambrano, E., Garces, G., & Bejarano, N. (2009). In-service English teacher's beliefs about culture and language methodology: An exploratory research in Montaría. *ZonaProxima,* (11), 32–51.

Lukenchuk, A. (2006). Traversing the chiasms of lived experiences: Phenomenological illuminations for practitioner research. *Education Action Research, 4*(3), 423–435.doi:10.1080/09650790600847826

Mackey, A., Al-Khalil, M., Atanassova, G., Hama, M., Logan-Terry, A., & Nakatsukasa, K. (2007). Teachers' intentions and learners' perceptions about corrective feedback in the L2 classroom. *Innovation in Language Learning & Teaching, 1*(1), 129–152. doi:10.2167/illt047.0.

Madhany, A. N. (2007). Teaching Arabic with technology now: Word processing, e-mail, and the Internet. In K. WAHBA, Z. Taha, &L. England (Eds.), *Handbook for Arabic language teaching professionals in the 21st century* (pp. 295–304). Mahwah, NJ: Erlbaum.

McAlpine, D., & Dhonau, S. (2007). Creating a culture for the preparation of an ACTFL/NCATE. *Foreign Language Annals, 40*(2), 247–259.

McConachy, T. (2009).Raising sociocultural awareness through contextual analysis: Some tools for teachers. *English Language Teachers Journal, 63*(2), 116–125. doi:10.1093/elt/ccn018.

McDonough, S. (2007).Motivation in ELT. *English Language Teachers Journal, 61*(4), 369–371. doi:10.1093/elt/ccm056.

McLaren, A. (2007). Designing distance instruction for the Arab world linguistic and cultural consideration. *Distance Learning, 4*(3), 17–21.

Merriam, S. B. (1998). Qualitative research and case study applications in education. San Francisco, CA: Jossey-Bass.

Merriam, S. B., & Associates. (2002). *Qualitative research in practice:Examples for discussion and analysis.* San Francisco, CA: Jossey-Bass.

Merriman, W., & Nicoletti, A. (2008). Communicative-driven: Globalization and American education. *Educational Forum, 72,* 8–22.

Mitchell, C., & Vidal, K. (2001).Weighing the ways of the flow: Twentieth century language instruction. *Modern Language Journal, 85*(1), 26–38.

Modern Language Association. (2009). Available at http://www.mla.org/.

Montrul, S.(2008). Second language acquisition welcomes the heritage language learner: Opportunities of a new field. *Second Language Research, 24*(4), 487–506.

Moustakas, C. (1994). *Phenomenological research methods.* Thousand Oaks, CA: Sage.

Muir, P. (2007). Toward culture: Some basic elements of culture-based instruction in China's high schools. *Sino–US English Teaching, 4*(4), 38–43.

National Capital Language Resource Center. (2006). Available at http://www.arabick12.org/schools.html.

National Standards for Foreign Language Learning Project. (1996). *Standards for language learning: Preparing for the 21st century.* Lawrence, KS: Allen Press.

National Standards for Foreign Language Learning Project.(2000). *Standards for language learning in the 21st century.* Lawrence, KS: Allen Press.

National Standards in Foreign Language Education Project. (2006). *Standards for foreign language learning in the 21st century*(3rd ed.).Alexandria, VA: Author.

Nieto, S. (2008). Chapter 9: Culture and education. *Yearbook of the National Society for the Study of Education, 107*(1), 127–142. doi:10.1111/j.1744-7984.2008.00137.x

Nikitina, L. (2011). Creating an authentic learning environment in the foreign language classroom. *International Journal of Instruction, 4*(1), 33–46.

Oh, J., & Au, T. K.-F. (2005). Learning Spanish as a heritage language: The role of sociocultural background variables. *Language, Culture & Curriculum, 18*(3), 229–241.

Omaggio-Hadley, A. (2001). *Teaching language in context.* Boston, MA: Heinle & Heinle.

Ömer, K., & Ali, D. (2011). The effect of culture integrated language courses on foreign education. *US–China Education Review, 8*(3), 257–263.

Patton, M. Q. (2002). *Qualitative evaluation and research methods.* Thousand Oaks, CA: Sage.

Payne, M. (2007). Foreign language planning: Pupil choice and pupil voice. *Journal of Education, 37*(1), 89–109.

Pei-Hsuan, P. H. (2008). Why are college foreign language students' self-efficacy, attitude, and motivation so different? *International Education, 38*(1), 76–94.

Peters, M. A. (2009). Editorial: Heidegger, phenomenology, education. *Educational Philosophy and Theory, 41*(1), 1–6. doi:10.1111/j.1469-5812.2008.00516.x.

Ping, W. (2010). The National Standards for Foreign Language Learning: Where's the beef? A response to "Motivating students' foreign language and culture acquisition through web-based inquiry" by Levi Altstaedter & Jones. *Foreign Language Annals, 43*(4), 559–562. doi:10.1111/j.1944-9720.2010.0111.

Rahimi, N. M., Muda, N., Mahamoud, Z., & Mat The, K. S. (2009). Relationship between Arabic listening skills and motivation. *International Journal of Learning, 16*(5), 139–150.

Reynold, R.R., Howard, K. M., & Deak, J. (2009). Heritage language learners in first-year foreign language courses: A report of general data across learner subtypes. *Foreign Language Annals, 42*(2), 250–269.

Riazi, A. (2007). Language learning strategy use: Perceptions of female Arab English majors. *Foreign Language Annals, 40*(3), 433–440.

Richards, J., & Rodgers, T. (2001).*Approaches and methods in language teaching* (2nd ed.). England: Cambridge University Press.

Ridder, I., de, Vangehuchten, L., & Gomez, M.S. (2007). Enhancing automaticity through task-based language learning. *Applied Linguistics, 28*(2), 309–315.doi:10.1093/Applin/am1057.

Riley, K. A., Abu-Saad, I., & Hermes, M. (2005). Big change questions: Should indigenous minorities have the right to have their own education systems, without reference to national standard? *Journal of Educational Change, 6*, 177–189.doi:10.1007/s10833-005-3235-y.

RosiSolé, C. (2007). Language learners' sociocultural positions in the L2: A narrative approach. *Language & Intercultural Communication, 7*(3), 203–216. doi:10.2167/laic203.0.

Rubin, H. J., & Rubin, I. S. (2005).*Qualitative interviewing: The art of hearing data* (2nd ed.). Thousand Oaks, CA: Sage.

Ryding, K.C. (2006). Teaching Arabic in the United States. In K. Wahba, Z. Taha, & L. England (Eds.), *Handbook for Arabic language and teaching professionals in the 21st century* (pp. 13–20). Mahwah, NJ: Erlbaum.

Samimy, K. (2008). Achieving the advanced oral proficiency in Arabic: A case study. *Foreign Language Annals, 41*(3), 401–415.

Sarıçoban, A., &, G. (2011).The influence of target culture on language learners. *Journal of Language & Linguistics Studies, 7*(1), 7–17.

Sawaie, M. (2006). International Arabic language programs. In K. Wahba, Z. Taha, & L. England (Eds.), *Handbook for Arabic language and teaching professionals in the 21st century* (pp. 371–381). Mahwah, NJ: Erlbaum.

Sayadian, S., & Lashkarian, A. (2010). Investigating attitude and motivation of Iranian university learners toward English as a foreign language. *Contemporary Issues in Education Research, 3*(1), 137–147.

Schuetze, U. (2008). Exchanging second language messages online: Developing an intercultural communicative competence? *Foreign Language Annals, 41*(4), 660–673.
Schulz, R. A. (2006). Perspectives: Reevaluating communicative competence as a major goal in postsecondary language requirement course. *Modern Language Journal, 90,* 252–255.
Schulz, R. A. (2007). The challenge of assessing cultural understanding in the context of foreign language instruction. *Foreign Language Annals, 40*(1), 9–26.
Schulz, R. A., & Ganz, A. (2010). Developing professional consensus on the teaching of culture: Report on a survey of secondary and postsecondary German teachers. *Teaching German, 43*(2), 175–193. doi:10.1111/j.1756-1221.2010.00079.x.
Seelye, H. (1993). *Teaching culture: Strategies for inter-cultural communication* (3rd ed.). Lincolnwood, IL: National Textbook.
Sehlaoui, A.S. (2008). Language learning, heritage, and literacy in the USA: The case of Arabic. *Language, Culture and Curriculum, 21*(3), 280–291.
Seidel, J. V. (1998). *The ethnography* (4th ed.). Colorado Springs, CO: Qualis.
Shank, G. D. (2006). *Qualitative research: A personal skills approach* (2nd ed.). Upper Saddle River, NJ: Pearson.
Smeyers, P. (2008). Qualitative and quantitative research methods: Old wine in new bottles? On understanding and interpreting educational phenomena. *Paedagogica Historica: International Journal of the History of Education, 44*(6), 691–705.
Stake, R.E. (1995). *The art of case study research.* Thousand Oaks, CA: Sage.
Stake, R.E. (2000).Case studies. In N. K. Denzin & Y. S. Lincoln (Eds.), *Handbook of qualitative research* (2nd ed., pp. 435–454). Thousand Oaks, CA: Sage.
Steinhart, M. M. (2006). Perspectives: Breaching the artificial barrier between communicative competence and content. *Modern Language Journal, 90,* 258–262.
Su, Y. (2008). Promoting cross-cultural awareness and understanding: Incorporating ethnographic interviews in college EFL classes in Taiwan. *Educational Studies, 34*(4), 377–398. doi:10.1080/03055690802257150.
Sugita, M., & Takeuchio, O. (2010). What can teachers do to motivate their students? A classroom research on motivational strategy use in the Japanese EFL context. *Innovation in Language Learning & Teaching, 4*(1), 21–35.doi:10.1080/17501220802450470.
Swaffar, J. (2006). Perspectives: Terminology and its discontents: Some caveats about communicative competence. *Modern Language Journal, 90,* 246–249.
Swain, M., & Deters, P. (2007). New mainstream SLA theory: Expanded and enriched. *Modern Language Journal,91*(5), 820–836. doi:10.1111/j.1540-4781.20070071.x.
Taha, T. (2006). Arabic as a critical need: Foreign language in post-9/11 era: A study of students' attitudes and motivation. *Journal of Instructional Psychology, 34*(3), 150–160.

References

Tallon, M. (2009). Foreign language anxiety and heritage students of Spanish: A quantitative study. *Foreign Language Annals, 42*(1), 112–137.

Tang, Y. (2006). Beyond behavior: Goals of cultural learning in the second language classroom. *Modern Language Journal, 90*(1), 86–99.

Tercanlioglu, L. (2008). A qualitative investigation of pre-service English as a foreign language (EFL): Teacher opinions. *Qualitative Report, 13*(1), 137–150.

Teachers of English to Speakers of Other Languages.(n.d.).*Case-study guidelines.* Retrieved from http://www.tesol.org/s_tesol/sec_document.asp?cid=476&did=2153.

Thomas, M. (2005). Theories of second language acquisition: Three sides, three angles, three points. *Second Language Research, 21*(4), 393–414. doi:10.1191/0267658305sr258ra.

Thorne, S. (2005). Epistemology, politics, and ethics in sociocultural theory. *Modern Language Journal, 89*(3), 393–409. doi:10.1111/j.1540-4781.2005.00313.x.

Toncy, N. (2008). Behind the veil: An in-depth exploration of Egyptian Muslim women's lives through dance. *International Journal of Qualitative Studies in Education, 21*(3), 269–280.doi:10.1080/09518390801998320.

Toohey, K. (2006). Sociocultural contexts of language and literacy. *International Journal of Bilingual Education & Bilingualism, 9*(2), 278–280.

Turner, D. W., III. (2010). Qualitative interview design: A practical guide for novice investigators. *Qualitative Report, 15*(3), 754–760. Retrieved from http://www.nova.edu/ssss/Qr15-3/qid.pdf.

Turuk, M. (2008).The relevance and implications of Vygotsky's sociocultural theory in the second language classroom. *Annual Review of Education, Communication & Language Sciences, 5*244–262.

Van Mol, M. (2006). Arabic receptive language teaching: A new CALL approach. In K. Wahba, Z. Taha, & L. England (Eds.), *Handbook for Arabic language and teaching professionals in the 21st century* (pp. 305–316). Mahwah, NJ: Erlbaum.

Vygotsky, L.S. (1929). The problem of the cultural development of the child, II. *Journal of Genetic Psychology,* (36), 414–434.

Vygotsky, L.S. (1978). *Mind in society. The development of higher psychological processes.* Cambridge, MA: Harvard University Press.

Vygotsky, L.S. (1986). *Thought and language.* Cambridge, MA: MIT Press.

Vygotsky, L.S.(1987).The *collected works of L.S. Vygotsky: Vol.1, problems of general psychology. Including the volume Thinking and speech* (N. Minick, Trans.). New York, NY: Plenum.

Wen-Chi, V. W., & Pin-Hsiang, N. W. (2008). Creating an authentic EFL learning environment to enhance student motivation to study English. *Asian EFL Journal, 10*(4), 211–226.

Wilbur, M.L. (2007). How foreign language teachers get taught: Methods of teaching methods course. *Foreign Language Annals, 40*(1) 79–101.

Wilkerson, C. (2006). College faculty perceptions about foreign language. *Foreign Language Annals, 39*(2), 310–321.

Wingfield, M. (2006). Arab Americans: Into the multicultural mainstream. *Equity & Excellence in Education, 39,* 253–266.
Wong, G. T., & Chan, Z. Y. (2010). A qualitative study of work-related stress among male staff in Hong Kong's social welfare sector. *International Journal of Men's Health, 9*(3), 221–238.doi:10.3149/jmh.0903.221.
Xingsong, S. (2006).Gender, identity and intercultural transformation in language socialisation. *Language & Intercultural Communication, 6*(1), 2–17.
Yi, J., & Kellogg, D. (2006). Beneath higher ground: Vygotsky, Volosinov, and an archaeology of reported speech in primary EFL writing. *Language Awareness, 15*(1), 38–52.
Yi, Q. (2010). Culture understanding in foreign language teaching. *English Language Teaching, 3*(4), 58–61.
Yin, R. K. (2003). *Case study research: Design and methods* (3rd ed.). Thousand Oaks, CA: Sage.
Yin, R. K. (2009). *Case study research: Design and methods*(4th ed.). Los Angeles, CA: Sage.
Yuanfang, Y., & Bing, W. (2009).A study of language learning strategy use in the context of EFL curriculum and pedagogy reform in China. *Asia Pacific Journal of Education, 29*(4), 457–468.doi:10.1080/02188790903309041.
Zehr, M. (2006). Group publishes nation's first Arabic Standards. *Education Week, 25*(43), 7.
Zhang, J. (2009). Mandarin maintenance among immigrant children from the People's Republic of China: An examination of individual networks of linguistic contact. *Language, Culture & Curriculum, 22*(3), 195–213. doi:10.1080/07908310903308279.
Zhu, H. (2010). Approaches to culture teaching at college level in China. *US–China Foreign Language, 8*(4), 43–48.

INDEX

9/11 (September 11, 2001), xi, 1–2, 10–11, 13, 15, 25, 68
African American(s), xiii–xiv, 32–33, 47, 63
Al-Batal, M., 17–18, 75–76
Arab American(s), xi, 2–11, 13, 16–17, 25, 30–33, 39, 40, 47–48, 50–53, 55, 56, 58, 59, 66, 68, 69, 75–77, 79; immigration to United States, 47; students, 3, 9–11, 30, 59; teachers, 9, 50, 55
Arabic language, xi–xii, 2–11, 13–14, 16–22, 29–33, 39–45, 47–48, 50–60, 62–80; courses, 3–4, 16; history of teaching, 16; learning, xi–xii, 3–4, 6–8, 10–11, 13–14, 17–22, 29–33, 40, 43–44, 55–60, 62–63, 65, 68–80
Arabic National Standards, 6
Askham, P., 33
Au, T., 4, 26, 70
Axelon, B., 18

Bejarano, N., 32
Belnap, K., 16–18, 75–76
Brown, K., 25–26

Caldwell, L., 43
Calışkan, G., 71
Colombia, 32

Communication, xii–xiii, 3–4, 6–11, 19–20, 23–24, 26–27, 36, 55, 64, 68, 72–75, 78, 80 (*See also* Five Cs)
Communities, xiii, 15, 17, 21, 36, 55, 74, 78 (*See also* Five Cs)
Comparisons, xiii, 3–4, 7, 9–10, 19–22, 27, 36, 55, 68, 75, 78, 80 (*See also* Five Cs)
Connections, xiii, 3–4, 7, 9–10, 19–21, 36, 55, 68, 75, 78, 80 (*See also* Five Cs)
Creswell, J., 4, 39–48, 50–51, 67
cultural, xi–xiv, 1–11, 13–28, 31–33, 36–37, 39–42, 44, 47–48, 51–80; activities, 5, 26, 42, 54, 56–57, 59, 69, 71, 75; awareness, xi–xi, 4–7, 9, 11, 21, 27, 36, 39–40, 42, 44, 48, 52–54, 56, 58–63, 65–69, 71, 73, 75–77, 79
Cultures, xiii–xiv, 3–4, 7, 9–10, 13, 15, 19–22, 36, 55, 60, 62–65, 68, 75, 78, 80 (*See also* Five Cs)
Csizér, K., 31

dance and Muslim women, 33
Detroit, 16, 58 (*See also* Michigan)
Diaz–Greenberg, R., 6, 22, 32, 36, 44
Dörnyei, Z., 31

Dutch language, 15–16 (*See also* Netherlands)

English First Language (EFL), 30–31, 35–36
Egypt/Egyptian, 16, 33
Extra, G., xiii, 15–16, 21

Five C's, xiii (*See* individual entries for "Communication, Cultures, Connections, Comparisons, and Communities"
foreign language, 1–4, 6–11, 13–14, 16–32, 34–37, 40, 43, 47, 51, 55, 61–62, 67–70, 73–74, 76, 79; teachers, 10, 18–19, 24, 30–31
Foreign Language Classroom Anxiety Scale, 35
Fox, R., 6, 22, 32, 36, 44

Garces, G., 32
Gardner, R., xiv, 8, 27–30, 32, 37
Ghenghesh, P., 35

Hatch, J., 40–43, 45–46, 48, 66
history of teaching Arabic, 16

immigration of Arabs to United States, 47
Iranm 31
Iwamoto, D., 43

Kraehe, A.m 25–26
Kramsch, C., 15, 18

Lambrano, E., 32
language, xiii–xiv, xvi, 1–11, 13–45, 47–80; EFL, 30–31, 35–36; Mandarin, 2, 34; second, 11, 13–14, 28, 31, 36, 65, 71; Spanish, 2, 26, 30, 35, 64

Lebanon/Lebanese, 3, 16, 34, 47, 55
Lee, J., 17, 33, 77
Libya (*See also* Tripoli), 35
linguistic(s), xiii, 1, 3, 6–8, 11, 14–16, 18, 20–21, 23, 25–26, 28–32, 37, 39, 65, 69–70, 72–75, 78–80; outcomes, 6, 16, 28–29
Lorduy, D., 32, 52
Lukenchuk, A., 41

McConachy, T., 27
Merriam, S., 4–5, 33, 39–43, 45–46, 48, 51, 66
Michigan, 16, 77
Modern Language Association, 1–2
Morocco/Moroccan, 15–16
motives/motivation, x, 8, 14, 28–37, 72, 77–78
motivational strategies, 30
Muslim women and dance, 33

National Capital Language Resource Center, 1, 17
Netherlands (*See also* Dutch language), 15
nonlinguistic outcomes, 28–29

Oh, J., 26

perspectives, xii–xiii, 4, 7–9, 13, 20–22, 36, 39–41, 43, 59–60, 67–69, 72–74, 78–79 (*See also* Three Ps)
Pin-Hsiang, N., 36
practices, xiii, 3–4, 7–8, 10, 13, 15, 18, 20–22, 33, 34, 36–37, 43, 53, 55, 57–61, 67–69, 72–79 (*See also* Three Ps)
products, xiii, 4, 7–9, 13, 20–22, 31, 36, 43, 53, 59–60, 67–69, 72–75, 78–80 (*See also* Three Ps)

Qatar, 35

Riazi, A., 31, 35
RosiSolé, C., 26–27

Sarıçoban, A., 71
Sawaie, M., 18
Schulz, R., 4, 18–19, 72, 79
second language, 11, 13–14, 28, 31, 36, 65, 71
Seidel, J., 48–50
September 11, 2001 (*See* 9/11)
social, xii–xiv, 4, 6–8, 10–11, 14–15, 18, 21–28, 33, 36–37, 39–41, 48, 54, 57, 70–74, 79; change, 10, 73–74
sociocultural theory, xii, 6, 8, 11, 13–14, 23–27, 36–37, 70
socioeducational theory, xii, 8, 13–14, 23, 27, 70
Standards for Learning Arabic, 3, 10, 13, 19, 69
Swaffar, J., 18
Syria/Syrian, 16

Taha, T., 1, 14–15, 17
teaching Arabic, history of, 16
Thomas, M., 24
Three Ps, 13, 22, 36, 59, 60, 74 (*See also* individual entries for "practices, products, perspectives")
Tripoli, Libya, 35
Turkish language, 15–16
Turner, D., 40, 43–44, 51

Vygotsky; L. xii, 6, 8, 23–27, 37; sociocultural theory, xii, 6, 8, 11, 13–14, 23–27, 36–37, 70

Wen–Chi, V., 36
Wilbur, M., 19

Yagmur, K., 15–16

Yemenis, 16

zone of proximal development (ZPD), 6, 8, 24–26, 37

www.ingramcontent.com/pod-product-compliance
Lightning Source LLC
Chambersburg PA
CBHW031554300426
44111CB00006BA/314